Schizophrenia, Mental Illness, and Pastoral Care

A PERSONAL AND BIBLICAL PERSPECTIVE

Adam W. Lambdin

WESTBOW
PRESS®
A DIVISION OF THOMAS NELSON
& ZONDERVAN

Copyright © 2016 Adam W. Lambdin.

All rights reserved. No part of this book may be used or reproduced by any means, graphic, electronic, or mechanical, including photocopying, recording, taping or by any information storage retrieval system without the written permission of the author except in the case of brief quotations embodied in critical articles and reviews.

WestBow Press books may be ordered through booksellers or by contacting:

WestBow Press
A Division of Thomas Nelson & Zondervan
1663 Liberty Drive
Bloomington, IN 47403
www.westbowpress.com
1 (866) 928-1240

Because of the dynamic nature of the Internet, any web addresses or links contained in this book may have changed since publication and may no longer be valid. The views expressed in this work are solely those of the author and do not necessarily reflect the views of the publisher, and the publisher hereby disclaims any responsibility for them.

Any people depicted in stock imagery provided by Thinkstock are models, and such images are being used for illustrative purposes only. Certain stock imagery © Thinkstock.

Scripture taken from the NEW AMERICAN STANDARD BIBLE®, Copyright © 1960, 1962, 1963, 1968, 1971, 1972, 1973, 1975, 1977, 1995 by The Lockman Foundation. Used by permission.

ISBN: 978-1-5127-6884-8 (sc)
ISBN: 978-1-5127-6886-2 (hc)
ISBN: 978-1-5127-6885-5 (e)

Library of Congress Control Number: 2016920743

Print information available on the last page.

WestBow Press rev. date: 12/28/2016

To James Goullette, for our weekly phone calls when I was schizophrenic and your encouragement in the midst of my delusions regarding sound doctrine and for encouraging me to have a love for Christ above all else. I am still uplifted by few others more than you.

Acknowledgments

I would like to acknowledge Bethany Baptist Church for the endless encouragement and all the love and support through the recent years. I also want to specifically acknowledge Dr. Lynne Boone for her contribution to the book as well as Pastor Craig Bowen for writing the preface. I also must acknowledge Janice Hargrave for painting me an awesome cover image. It has certainly been a family-of-God production. Thank you.

Contents

Preface xi
Foreword xiii

Exploring the Issues

Chapter 1   Not Defining Normality, Just the Nature of Schizophrenia 1

My Experience with Schizophrenia

Chapter 2   An "Ingrown Toenail" of the Body of Christ 9
Chapter 3   I'm Unplugging the Matrix, Neo 19

The Ins and Outs of Schizophrenia and Its treatment

Chapter 4   The Biological Basis of Schizophrenia 35
Chapter 5   Therapy Versus Soul Care 51

What We as Laymen and Ministers Can Do for Them

Chapter 6   Meditation and the Nature of Mental Illness 67
Chapter 7   The Encouragement That a Schizophrenic Needs from the Bible 73

Bibliography 93

Preface

One of my favorite genres of literature is autobiography. We read the stories of our heroes to know them better and to profit from their hard-learned lessons. Adam's story is a brief but valuable recounting of his own descent into schizophrenia and the difficult path back to normalcy. Adam's journey was uniquely complicated, protected and finally enriched by his deeply held Christian faith. Complicated because traditional Christian counseling is reluctant to accept schizophrenia as a medical condition. Protected because God promises to keep His own, and God preserved Adam through some dark days. Enriched because Adam has regained normalcy and has worked to evaluate his journey in the light of scripture, while often at odds with the consensus views of the Christian counseling community. There are lessons to be learned from Adam's journey.

Adam's insights are important to me because my calling is to provide soul care, specifically to provide soul care to Adam and his family. I became Adam's pastor (and his parents' pastor) as he was beginning his climb back to the real world. I knew little about schizophrenia. My counseling training taught that problems like Adam's were almost always sin problems. But even my limited small-town, small-church counseling experience had left me wondering if some people's behavioral problems were really only sin problems. If man and his brain are fearfully and wonderfully made, and if his brain and his soul are intertwined, then maybe his brain can fall prey to medical problems we have yet to fully understand. And maybe in such states sin is allowed freer reign in his flesh. As Adam confesses, "I had a sinful heart and a broken mind ... My insanity had simply uncovered my sin hidden in my heart ..."

I've learned a lot about schizophrenia and counseling from my friendship with Adam. Yet his story reminds me that there is a lot about ourselves we still don't understand. And even when our problems require medical intervention, the truth of scripture and the love of family and friends constitute a powerful medicine in the lives of God's children.

Sincerely,

Craig Bowen
Adam's friend and pastor

Foreword

The shuffled gait of a homeless man pushing a shopping cart along the crosswalk arrests our vision. We sit through the green light, willing him to make it across the street without being clipped by a too-hurried motorist. Our parallel thoughts accuse him, *He must be an alcoholic*, or blame the system that fails to provide him adequate shelter. We reflect, momentarily, on sleeping under bridges and scrounging for food from trash cans. He catches our eye again as he nears the corner, edging his cart up the dirty easement. He begins to scream and shake his fist at the sky and then charges into traffic, pounding on car windows as the traffic lurches around him. We slip out of the tangle of cars, carefully avoiding his grimy fists as he lunges at unseen foes. The experience leaves us shaken, wondering who the man used to be and why he is the way he is.

The thought of mental illness is unsettling, and we do not understand it. After all, we're lying down on clean sheets at night, thinking orderly thoughts and thanking God for his kindness. We see the benefits of hard work, honest living, and a strong community. We order and found our lives on the great truths of the Bible and live predictably within our fortresses. Our theology is airtight, and our belief schemas intact.

But what if the enemy is within, insidious? What if, stealing across our pillow in the moonlight, come dark thoughts and aberrations? What if they keep coming, not just once but nightly? And what if they cross our threshold during the day, beginning all at once or slowly, to tell us whisperingly, strangely, believably that the person lying next to us has a black heart, ulterior motives, and has been deceiving us all along? And at the breakfast table, although they look and act the same as they always did, they aren't really that person they pretend to be? Shaking this off is easy at first, but then the proof mounts. A letter stuffed in the mailbox at an angle is a sign that things are not as they seem. The pastor at church uses certain verses in his sermon. They're a message about your family member. The sermon is something about love, but you hear what he's really saying, loud and clear. He's using a secret form of communication and speaking directly to you, corroborating your nascent feelings that what you're seeing is all an illusion and that you shouldn't be deceived. The pastor is feeling the same way! And then God speaks to you and tells you that "things are not what they look like." You sense the warning and the danger. The world as you have known it is not real. It's like a painting on cardboard, placed in front of a window, blocking what is actually there. The truth is out there, and you are the one that will uncover it and save millions of lives.

"Seek for truth as silver," you read in the Bible. So, you sneak out that night and walk around the perimeter of your house, not once but all night long. You sense the pulsing, breathing evil around you, inhabiting every shadow. You know you're not wrestling against flesh and blood but that these are spiritual forces. When the threatening breathing takes the form of words, you whisper Bible verses to them. When they begin to poke you and jab at you, you strike at them with your hands, rebuking them in the name of Jesus. Eventually you're shouting at them. This wakes the neighbors, who call the police. It's then that you realize that everyone, all of them, are under a strong delusion and you alone are seeing the truth. These people around you are all imposters, and the police need to know about it! Maybe they can help. Maybe they already know the truth themselves.

The police, for their part, try to be respectful and calm you down, but you grow more agitated, shouting at them and your family that they are not full of truth but lies. You wave your Bible around and start praying out loud on your knees in the middle of your yard. When you're interrupted, you begin gesticulating wildly at the officers. They perceive it as a threat and Taze you. With wide eyes, your family stares at you, watching you be taken away, handcuffed, in a police car with an involuntary hold written against you. The hold states that you are dangerous to others and mentions words like "unpredictable" and "labile" and "paranoid" and "aggressive." They take you to the nearest psychiatric emergency room.

This is where I meet you.

As a psychiatry resident in Southern California, I have seen this scenario multiple times. I have been on the receiving end of this hyper-religious, paranoid patient, with ideas of reference and grandiose delusions. The presence of a Bible in the hand of psychiatric patient is always, strangely, a bad sign.

No one would question this presentation when substance abuse is involved and a person is under the influence of drugs or alcohol. But what if that isn't the reason? And what if the person is a believer, with a grasp of the truth, a responsible job, and who has for years sat next to you in church?

Where does our theology go when confronted with this reality? Our understanding of the intricacy of the body, mirrored a thousand-fold in the mind, points to an orderly Creator with an exquisite sense of design. When the body breaks down through age, disease, or traumatic injury, we understand it widely as a direct result of the fall. But when the mind breaks down, not through an age-acquired illness like dementia or through traumatic brain injury as in a motor vehicle accident, do we view it differently? And is our understanding of it as just a spiritual issue a primitive one? Would we have looked at the stuffed asylums in the 1920s, full of staggering psychotic patients, as the domain of especial spiritual darkness, when in fact, penicillin would have prevented their neurosyphilis completely?

Is it possible that we are not fully cognizant of the deleterious effects of the fall, not only on our bodies but even on our brain and therefore our mind? We now know that Alzheimer's disease can, for a time, be stayed by an acetylcholine-esterase inhibitor because cholinergic neurons are diminished in the diseased brain. We know that blood pressure medications, namely alpha2-agonists like clonidine, can help control the agitation and intense anxiety that is experienced by autistic children. Seizures, once thought to be demonic possession only, can be addressed by the family of anti-convulsant medications.

Schizophrenia, then, may be understood to have a biological basis; indeed, it is the most observed heritable disease and the mental illness that we have studied the most. It affects 1 percent of the population across the world, regardless of nation, ethnicity, or religion and effects a downward drift, with functional people ending up, without treatment, often as the homeless man who bisected our vision to begin this introduction.

Mind and body, soul and spirit—made in the image of the Creator, ruined and riddled by sin and its wages! As a physician, my best work is when the Great Physician's hand encloses mine. I chart my patient encounters; the prescriptions, the therapy referrals. I witness continual transformations, series of miracles really, as dopamine-blocking agents restore organization to disordered minds. Families reunite—the problem member is welcomed home. Their sleep becomes regular, since they are not afraid anymore to lie down. Their children are safer. No longer does their parent believe the devil is inside them. The streets benefit—no longer is the paranoid person attacking others, thinking they are being stalked. And occasionally, as their thoughts become linear and some insight creeps back in, patients tell me of their church attendance and their Bible studies. I discreetly inquire about what they're studying and where their church is. I hope against all hope that their pastors are truly godly and preaching the truth.

Adam's account of his first psychotic break and subsequent schizophrenia diagnosis is riveting. The insight he has been given as he views his illness both retrospectively and prospectively is unusual. And his fervent desire to honor God with his mind, diagnosed as it is, makes these following chapters even more compelling.

May our God use this honest and sometimes painful account for our edification! May He give us wisdom and understanding and knowledge as we attempt to study and learn more together about that fearful and wonderful intersection of the soul and the brain.

Dr. Lynne D. Boone
Psychiatry Resident, PGY-4
San Bernardino, CA

PART 1
Exploring the Issues

CHAPTER 1

Not Defining Normality, Just the Nature of Schizophrenia

How do we deal with schizophrenia and schizophrenics? The issue is harder to understand than a person might think. Can we use biblical or pastoral counseling? Yes, I would say, but there is a lot more understanding that needs to go into our nonclinical treatment than we might assume. It is very difficult to just go for the jugular, so to speak, in a counseling scenario with persons suffering with this illness. It actually requires an overflow of patience, and then respect and kindness in great measure. The greatest thing that a pastor or counselor might offer is the relationship of support and listening and interacting like you should with any rational person.

When is a person not sinful? And how do we understand and deal with sin in a schizophrenic's life? Are normal people not sinful anymore when they sleep? How about when we are not dreaming and sleep is just an utter unconscious black? When are we ever not sinful? The answer is never. Is being clinically delusional a deeper, more severe form of sin? Another way of putting this is to ask if believing things that are patently false according to the "other 99 percent of humanity" (1 percent of the population is schizophrenic) is particularly sinful.

How does this compare and contrast with everyday persons who vary in their fundamental religious, moral, philosophical, or practical beliefs all of the time? We want to deal with all these things, but we rarely call these people delusional unless as a means of insult. In a sense, we are all wrong in our beliefs on some level. A person could argue about whether or not people are ever not delusional on some level rather than to answer the question of when is a person ever normal. Normality is subjective and is based on various assumptions about what normality looks like. Philosophers and sociologists and all kinds of whatever other "ologists" have debated the definition of normal for centuries. I do not believe that we can define normal or abnormal at all except on pragmatic terms or based on whatever definition does the most good for the most people. And that overflows into our treatment of schizophrenia as well on some level.

On the other hand, "delusional," as a word, actually carries a greater weight because it is less subjective when thought of in extreme cases such as in schizophrenia. Obviously, there are delusional persons. I would argue that there are many more spiritually delusional persons than there are clinically delusional psychotics, but what makes people delusional is not their spiritual error but their insistence on believing something despite all evidence to the contrary. They believe something that is so obviously false despite all the proofs in the world, yet I believe that there can be spiritually sound psychotics or Christians.

At the same time, I understand that there is an organization that actually believes that the world is really flat and that all of the photographs of earth from orbit are fabricated lies. Should we start calling these persons psychotic? Undoubtedly some smart aleck would reply that probably a lot of the members of this organization could have psychotic diagnoses, and he would probably be right on some level, but there are people undoubtedly sane in this organization as well.

My point is: why waste time obsessing over correcting the sinfulness of delusional thinking in a psychotic when we can't even define, as biblical or pastoral counselors, what "normal" is in the strictest sense? Well, we can take pains to help persons with their wrong patterns of thought in understanding and respectful ways, but why obsess over the actual sinfulness of it when we can't even clearly divide the difference between what is caused by warped brain matter, so to speak, and what is caused by spiritual rebellion? The brain is an amazing mystery. Dr. Allen Frances writes:

> The human brain is by far the most complicated thing in the known universe. The brain has 100 billion neurons, each of which is connected to 1,000 other neurons—making for a grand total of 100 trillion synaptic connections. Every second, an average of 1,000 signals cross each of these synapses; each signal is modulated by 1,500 proteins and mediated by one or more of dozens of neurotransmitters. Brain development is even more improbable—a miracle of intricately choreographed sequential nerve cell migration. Each nerve has to somehow find just its right spot and make just the right connections. Given all the many steps involved and all the possible things that can go wrong, you might want to place your bet on Murphy's Law and chaos theory—the odds seem to be stacked against normal brain functioning. The weird and wonderful thing is that we work as well as we do—the improbable result of exquisitely wrought DNA engineering that has to accomplish trillions and trillions of steps. But any supercomplicated system will have its occasional chaotic glitches. Things can and do go wrong in many different ways to produce each disease, which makes it hard for medical science to take giant steps.[1]

There is so much happening each second in a human brain and so much developing in a growing child that there could be insane

---

[1] Allen Frances, *Saving Normal* (New York, New York: HarperCollins Publishers, 2013), 10.

numbers of things happening or going wrong at any time, which makes it virtually impossible to know what is going wrong in all the vast numbers of mental illnesses and brain diseases that are out there. The bottom line is that we simply do not know where to divide sin from warped biology in mental illness. I am, however, not talking about alcoholism, which does not have very much support for being an illness, but about schizophrenia. What is brain disease? Science has so much to grow in and to learn about that we continue to develop all the time. The answers are coming slowly but surely. I greatly hope to know what causes schizophrenia in my own brain by the end of my lifetime.

There is a lot in the secular world that is excused as illness that shouldn't be, on the one hand, and there is a lot that we are gradually learning about, especially in the traditional biblical counseling community, that does not need to be seen as sin, on the other hand. Mental illness is not a bad word. A pragmatic approach to the vast terminologies for each "mental illness" needs to be taken into consideration. Of course the term "mental illness" is overused, and sin is over-excused, but let's not go too far in the other direction.

I believe that there is just too much about the human brain that we do not understand. I believe that because of that, we should take a less certain stance in whatever direction we lean. When dealing with people, already confused people, we could lead them to conclude any vast number of narratives regarding their suffering. They could adopt a number of our convictions and make them their own and fill in their newly adopted paradigm with all the events of their lives and make it convincing. My book is not about doing that. I am not writing to fit what I am saying into a perspective on mental illness. I am writing to share with you the basics of what we do know, what I have been through myself, and what we can do as ministers of the gospel.

This does not mean at all that sin is not present. We are never not sinful. We are always wrestling with this body of death just as Paul did in Romans 7. As biblical and pastoral counselors, we know that sin is there. There is just no reason to assume that sin is the cause of psychosis, or even a partial cause at whatever points. We simply do not know. I do not have a problem with individual sufferers coming to the conclusion that sin may have been the cause or a contributing factor in some way to their worsening delusional thinking patterns. That is certainly possible, but pastoral counselors should rid themselves of presumptions on this point and allow the counselee to come to this conclusion on their own, assuming that they are not delusional in these points as well.

Guilt is still guilt, and anxiety is still anxiety. Anger is still anger, but it may help to know that in a schizophrenic person, the anger that they might demonstrate may be void of emotion (called lack of affect) and they are simply interacting with their delusions and the way that they perceive other people. Voices could be telling them to act out, or Martians could be controlling them. That's not an excuse. It's a delusion. So deal with sin but make sure that, as such, you are not confusing sin with delusion. The difference is where the physical meets the spiritual, or where the body and the soul interact and depend on one another. You may not know where all to divide the issues of sin from the brain chemistry, but the soul is obviously in the works and needs guidance, not just correction.

Have I confused you enough? This spirit, or heart, or inner man, as we say in theology class, is inseparable from that lump of gray matter in our cranial cavity while we live together with it. Descartes believed that it was located in the pineal gland of the brain, but there is no way that we cannot say that the soul is bound and even inhibited by the physical brain and body or this theological "flesh" as the Bible refers to it.

When we are tired, we oftentimes become irresistibly irritable, even if we don't show it. When we are hungry, we become anxious for food and so forth. So a person can conceive of the fact that when our brains limit us and when it is damaged, as in severe brain trauma, we are generally much more character deficient in the sense that our brain matter has been made insufficient not because of a lack of food or sleep but because of literally damaged tissue. This is testified to in the vast number of those who suffer from brain trauma from car accidents or from warfare, for example. Families say that their family member has never been the same since. Is it absolutely impossible to improve? No. But it is very difficult and can possibly only go so far.

Schizophrenia is essentially biological in nature, though genetically vulnerable individuals may not get schizophrenia due to a lack of the right environmental stressors or other factors in their development before birth, for example. The following variations exist among others: There is paranoid schizophrenia, which is characterized by paranoia of other people being out to get them. Catatonic schizophrenia is characterized by a person becoming rigid and not moving. There is disorganized schizophrenia, which is characterized by the patient's lack of ability to create understandable and logical thoughts. Then there is undifferentiated schizophrenia, which may meet the general characteristics of delusions or hearing and seeing things as well as a loss of affect (which means the loss of the ability to feel or to express emotions), but it does not fit with any of the main characteristics of the previous classifications, so it is sort of a catch-all for the other cases. This happens to be my own diagnosis. Along these lines, schizoaffective disorder is also a less precisely defined illness, but while it may have delusions and hallucinations (seeing or hearing things), it is also characterized by mood disorder. Then there is schizotypal disorder, which is characterized by having strange or eccentric beliefs and being out of touch with people, unable to form healthy relationships.

Schizophrenia is a serious medical condition and most often destroys the lives of those who have it. There is hope for treatment, and there is encouragement from friends and loved ones and pastoral counselors, but patience is the key ingredient. My following chapters are about educating people about this condition and correcting misconceptions, which in turn will lead to better help coming from pastors and family. I will share my own story here for understanding's sake and in order to relate to those who have this disease.

PART 2
My Experience with Schizophrenia

CHAPTER 2

An "Ingrown Toenail" of the Body of Christ

My schizophrenia really began when I was about twenty years old, as far as I can tell. I was attending my local community college, and I started to become highly suspicious that people were out to get me. At one point, I thought that someone drew a target in the rain droplets on my car while it was parked in the parking lot at the college. I didn't really look very closely because I didn't want people to think that I noticed it, but I firmly believed it. I started to notice scratches and such on the car as well, which I believed people had put there while I was at work at McDonald's.

California

I started to go through just the general culture shock of adapting to life outside of the homeschool bubble, not that that is inherently a bad thing, and I became very depressed at times because of the general workload of twenty-seven hours a week at McDonald's and doing twelve units at the college. I rarely sat down and enjoyed a movie with my family anymore. Anyway, I dreamed of going to The Master's College and studying the Bible there, so I packed my things as soon as I received my acceptance letter and moved out to California to live with my grandparents while I was supposed to take one class that first semester in the fall of 2004.

The McDonald's in Palmdale, California, was my first job there, and school started soon afterward. By the time November came around, I was trying to find a job that could pay a little more, or at least work a little better with school. I was shortly thereafter working overnights stocking shelves for the holiday season at Wal-Mart.

When I ended my shift at Wal-Mart after Christmas night, I found out that I had been whittled out from the work group and sent on. Not that that wasn't supposed to have happened, as it was a temporary job, but I took it hard.

My Beginning Condition

Back on September 11, 2004, I began the process to be a deputy sheriff for LASD. I'm not sure how I saw myself as anywhere near ready for something like that, but for whatever reason, I spent the following five months going in and out of filling out paperwork and doing meetings. I struggled with a sense of being followed all the while. I was generally very depressed and lonely because I had very few friends and very little contact because I worked overnights and went to school and really was not connected with family either.

I remember that at about the time I moved out of my grandparents' house because I was not getting along with my grandpa very well, I was reading St. Augustine's *Confessions*. I really related to the intense spiritual introspection of Augustine. I really believed that I was comparable to the Reformers or the great men of church history like Augustine because of the intensity of my own spiritual longings and so forth. Looking back, I suppose that that was my own kind of delusion of grandeur.

My emotions did go through highs and lows a lot. There is such a thing as schizophrenic with bipolar tendencies, and that could very well be me. I would go into deep depression and loneliness (often the two went hand in hand), and then I would experience more brief highs of elation where I believed no one could get to me.

The job front continued just as it did before then. I had to make money and learn about how to work with people at the same time, which was multitasking as far as I was concerned. When one job ended because I left, or usually because I was having trouble, I got another one. Ministry was something that I didn't care about so much and really couldn't do anyway with all of my problems.

Moving to and Fro

Moving out of my grandparents' place and into a place farther away from the college soon after wasn't really a part of my goals, but I moved in with a bunch of great guys. I just didn't have the ability to connect with them. Having had such a conservative background for one thing, I snubbed their goofiness, I suppose, but I did go out with them on a couple events that I really was able to enjoy.

There would be two more roommate situations, and the time at my new job at a garage remodeling company got more difficult, and balancing work and school was not the easiest thing in the world. It came down to the foreman talking with me again about not listening or following through with directions. I was obviously not doing a good job. I felt fed up. After all, I had absolutely no clue that I was schizophrenic and was thus struggling with listening to people because I was mentally sick. As I would learn about myself later from a VA intelligence test, I am not the kind of person who multitasks very well. If I was hearing voices in my head, then I couldn't really focus on anything else for the simple reason that my attention was divided.

Anyway, I did not want to change jobs again on my work history, but I knew at that time that there was an opening at the college for another security spot, and it offered tuition reimbursement, so I moved again, closer to the college. It was all about getting that BA in Christian ministry and becoming the next great church leader or something.

I worked there at The Master's College for the following year and a half but had to deal with four write-ups during this time. Two involved being late to work and two frustrated encounters with individuals on campus. One involved asking a coworker out a third time after being warned not to be in the office at all. The last involved failing to unlock a door. They were fed up with me by this point and rightly so. They basically asked me to find another job in six months and move on, which I did. I remember not even really believing that they were going to actually make me leave after six months. I could hear them telling me through subtle gestures and so forth that it would all just be forgotten, and I would not have to leave anyway. The ways that I reasoned were incredibly out of touch, and I simply had no idea.

The Tension

In these preceding years, I struggled a lot with depression, as I have already said, and as is often the case with Christians, this meant doubting my salvation. There were three separate bouts I had when I had a strong sense of loneliness and depression that would hit me. My very stupid response was to look at God and wonder why, if in fact life was sizing up to be so pathetic for me with all of these people problems, was there even in my life a real relationship with God at all? I had heard people say to me, in response to all of my problems, that when your relationship with others is bad, it is an indicator that your relationship with God is also bad. That compounded my burden exponentially because I then doubted that I had a relationship with God.

Imagine being schizophrenic when no one knew it, not even you, and relationships are going down all around you, and someone tells you that relationships with other people is an indicator of your relationship with God. It was bewildering, and it brought me to tears. I felt like the sincerest person in the world, however I seemed to others. My conscience always vindicated me because I knew that I prayed sincerely all the time that God would make me a man after His own heart, and I believed that and pursued it. I just struggled to connect with other people or understand them because they told me one thing in person, but I always warped in my mind what they actually told me into something else.

Beyond this, the only reason I could find for my sense of separation from others was my guilt and bad judgment. The result of all this was depression, which unfortunately led me to talk to counselors in my life about whether or not I really had done what I needed to do to have a real relationship God. At this point, I was not yet hearing voices as audibly as I would later. I pretty much read into other people's gestures and intonations of voice at this point, and I warped what they said into something entirely different.

I seemed to gain some sense of victory over the deep depression that I experienced so often at the beginning. I was counseled often enough, and I read C.J. Mahaney's *The Cross Centered Life*. These two things and perhaps some other books I was reading in school and so forth did have some positive effects. I really didn't struggle for a couple years with the same heavy depression that I had before then from 2007 till my entrance into the army, where it got worse.

Always Moving On

After leaving the school as a security guard, I went and did some temporary work as a janitor at Grace Community Church for two months before starting at a small company as an inventory clerk in September 2007. I determined that at ten dollars an hour, I was going to work as hard as possible and succeed at this job for sure. I was never a day late, I was never caught standing, and I tried to come up with some different ways of organizing all the stuff that the company had laying around. I never received a write-up in fact, though maybe I should have. During this time, one thing happened at both work and the apartment. My relationships with people were all turning south all the more. At work, I was criticized for not listening. At the apartment, I was criticized for not relating to people as I should, not spending enough time with the guys, or for just forgetting to do the dishes.

It was while I was working as an inventory clerk that one day I heard my boss speak to me while I was in the warehouse. The only problem was that he was in the office behind a closed door. I heard him say hello, and he introduced me to speaking and listening inside one's head. I remember asking him why I had never heard of this before, and he said that no one had taught me. It was something that one's parents were supposed to teach a person. My parents had cut me loose in the world without a proper education in extrasensory perception! I was shocked to hear him say that that was the reason why I couldn't be accepted anywhere. Again, this was all just my own thoughts. That was the reason I was having so much trouble with relationships. I couldn't be allowed to succeed in the world without a "proper education" in speaking to people in my head or telepathically. I was in a sense relieved at the time to learn that none of this had actually been my fault! I was being rejected by society and job after job and home after home, but it was not my fault. It was all of a sudden, and this was a major revelation to me there while at work that day. Again, this was all the thought processes inside my own head. I was hearing voices much more than I had before when I was just at the college as a security guard, where I barely heard voices.

Finding my roommate sleeping in his bed back at the apartment, I excitedly told him, in my head, that I could speak now. I remember very clearly the intense stress at the same time. I was very stressed having to keep up conversations in my head to everyone that I was around all the time. Everyone talked to me about my future and what was going to happen. I had no idea how mentally sick I was. I had no idea that talking to people through my own thoughts was not even real at this point. I was getting more and more mentally sick, and I had no idea, while I thought I was slowly becoming more and more enlightened and acceptable to others.

I oftentimes imagined that this had been placed in my life to make me great, and I was being trained for such greatness through this great humiliation, as it were. I was being made worthy through suffering. At first, I pictured all of the preachers on Sunday, including John MacArthur, gesturing in their subtle ways or their intonations of speech to communicate and answer me indirectly while they preached. I was taking everything personally. Who could miss it? It consoled me in the midst of my defeat and affliction that I was going through in relationships. I was special.

One individual at church, to whom I was proclaiming (in a real conversation) all the failures and errors of my roommates, said that he had met lots of people like himself and like me who were the "ingrown toenails of the body of Christ." No one had ever called me one of the "ingrown toenails of the church" before, as funny as that is now to me. But I see his point in retrospect. It just totally offended me at the time.

It got to the point with my current roommates that I needed to leave the apartment or submit to counseling from an elder in our local area Bible study with the college ministry at the church. I was never spending time with my roommates, which was their main objection, and I rarely cleaned up around the apartment. There were some things that I said and did that were somewhat odd, and I know that that must have had an influence on them as well.

Criticism

The demands of work and school were enough to keep me busy, but the personal criticism was a lot to bear. One of them tended to head the criticism, though in a kind way, and he talked from even a rather compassionate standpoint about relating to people and the importance of being a part of the rest of the guys, as I said above. There was too much for me to deal with personally, and I expressed that to them. All I said, that I could say at this point, was that I must have been in the wrong. I just couldn't think of what else to say. So I acknowledged what I had to assume was my strong sense of guilt, but I just couldn't ever bring myself to change.

From my impoverished perspective, I could talk about cleaning, or even hanging out with the guys, which seemed to be the main reason for their objection about me, but being anywhere but studying at my desk sounded useless to me. All my time was wrapped up in work, and I wanted it that way. Reclusiveness is a key characteristic of a schizophrenic person, though none of us had any idea that that was what was wrong. At the same time, I honestly did not value people either. If you're going to be a hard worker with no real time for society, you could at least still value people enough to regret that you couldn't fellowship more, but I was rather disgusted with them. It was ironic that I wanted to be a pastor. Maybe that was the problem my roommates could see in me but that I didn't care about really.

At work, the criticism kept getting tougher as well. I lost a device that was used to stamp the company seal on all the parts. I was not remembering different requests or even writing them down, as I had been asked to do by the others. My last day started with me nicking the back passenger bumper of a coworker's vehicle with the company truck. It was my fault, and I volunteered to pay for it, but they understandably had had enough and terminated my employment that day.

Perhaps one to two months before then, as I mentioned above, I had begun to hear voices in my head talking to me. No one else would know this for two more years because I didn't say anything, but I was constantly talking to other people in the room through my newfound "extrasensory perception." I was going crazy really, if I can be allowed to call myself "crazy" for schizophrenia. It doesn't seem to be the acceptable or politically correct term for schizophrenics. At the same time, my thoughts were very wrong.

To backtrack a bit, the dramatic climax to my troubles at the apartment a couple of months later was when I got personally vindictive and set the alarm clock at the same time as I was being kept up by my roommate's snoring and just left the alarm running repeated times to get back at him. I envisioned everyone as trying to "stop me." Even my roommate's snoring was his effort to try to keep me awake. So, I was vindictive back to him. My roommates had had enough of me and asked me to leave for various reasons.

All the while, I saw it as my responsibility to fight for my right to be accepted in society as a whole. Eventually, I would learn through talking in my head to people that I had to keep going and keep being rejected—again, delusional thoughts of grandeur. On the other hand, I went through times of incredible depression and feeling defeated as I thought of how miserable I was. "I was a reject." I believed that everyone was waiting for me to learn this. At the same time, they were coaxing me along as I failed. I always had the option of returning home to Mom and Dad, but the thought was offensive to my sense of manhood and independence, and I didn't want to be defeated. I preferred to live life in my misery and be continually hurt by everyone. I wanted to sacrifice myself in my religious fervor. All my thoughts revolved around me like a prison.

I agreed to my roommates' demands that I leave and started looking for another place, not that I didn't say a few more cryptically strange and schizophrenic things, which appeared to them as anger but really were not angry for me (loss of affect) on my way out the door. I had the ability to appear angry without feeling angry. I called one of them a name, for example, which was based on my false perception of him. Society has strange rules in a schizophrenic's mind. I, as a schizophrenic, thought that I was following them, the rules that we all talked about in our heads through extrasensory perception but were too polite to talk about out loud, except for the people who couldn't take it but let it all out—and got locked up in psych wards because they couldn't keep their mouths shut. I had completely lost my mind.

CHAPTER 3

I'm Unplugging the Matrix, Neo

I called this chapter what I did because the end involves me beginning to recover. I don't need to get into all the details of life or my delusions, as that would be abysmally embarrassing. I really do omit a lot of very awful stuff that I had to deal with, but it gets the point across. Anyway, being schizophrenic for me involved delusions of grandeur to a certain degree. If I had seen a movie like *The Matrix*, I would have presumed that in some mysterious way it was about me. That's just how far out I was.

Oftentimes, yours truly was "the one," and at other times still locked up in the Matrix even though I had taken the pill, so to speak, in order to get out of it. I just couldn't escape my own mind.

All the while, my uncle James was the most encouraging person in my life at the time, and he gave me a lot of encouragement to love Christ, reject self, and trust in sound doctrine. James is what convinces me that biblical counseling can be a massive aid in encouraging and uplifting a schizophrenic mind. I cannot emphasize enough how I would have given up or failed in other ways had James not been there to pick up the emotional wreck that I was and set me on the straight and narrow toward Christ even though my delusions were so dominating. He repeated very often that God would complete the good work that He had started in me, and he told me how natural it was for me to feel terrible about myself because of sin. I didn't need self-esteem. I needed to see myself in light of the fact that when God sees me, He now sees the perfection of Christ, and when God looks at Christ, He sees all my sins atoned for perfectly because of His death on the cross. Pure and simple Christian doctrine is the most encouraging thing imaginable for a guilty soul.

Rejected All the More

I temporarily moved up again to be with my grandparents for two months while working at a security company and looking for some new roommates. While there, I graduated from the college. I found a place up in Sylmar with some new roommates. Turning in my application, I was denied at the seminary due to my relationship problems with other roommates and so forth. I talked with my Bible study leader about rejoining Grace Community Church, which I had randomly decided to withdraw my membership from, in retaliation.

Having quit my membership there, I wanted to continue to push back at all those who were "wronging me" at church. I had a Bible study leader there whose problem with me was that I was not faithful to stay at the study and be discipled for the problems that I was having with my former roommates and so on.

Having agreed to be discipled previously, it lasted not more than a month. All this had happened back when I was still living with the roommates whom I had lasted with the longest while in the area. I felt disconnected from the study and honestly ashamed of the whole situation at home and at work and everywhere.

My counselor (the elder from the Bible study in the previous chapter) was an MA in biblical counseling student. He had approached my problems from the perspective of relationships in my life and how I needed to work on that because my problems revolved around relating to people.

But I had rejected all his efforts to help by now. I began to struggle with loss of sleep and for a definite two week stretch was up for at least two hours or more after returning home at 12:45 a.m. from work as a security guard at another company. I had the worst time sleeping on Saturday nights, which left me too tired to go to church the next morning. I began to drop off from being connected with people at all. At the same time, I began to get very strange adrenaline rushes that set me to instant screaming and throwing things at times. All this, I assumed, was controlled by other people, even from very far away. I believed that there were cameras in every room watching me, and people could, even remotely, push a button and cause me to go haywire. On my way out the door to work one time, I whipped my belt sidearm into the railing, and the buckle flew off and broke the window in the stairway. At other times, I began randomly grabbing the walls and started screaming. Another time, I picked up a cup and threw it into the wall, breaking it and putting a large hole in the wall.

Again, I threw my fist on different occasions into the walls, scraping and causing them to bleed. These random outbursts, I would tell my landlord, were without any real direct cause to me at the time, at least not that I mentioned to people. I believed inside that others were causing it to happen in me, but if I had told them that, then they would have assumed I was crazy, so I didn't say it. I was schizophrenic and was pretty much getting worse all the time.

It was torture, especially since I didn't have any objective excuse for any of this because I wouldn't talk about my delusions to people. I was losing my grip on reality as a schizophrenic but remained silent. I simply did these things seemingly uncontrollably, and as I told my landlord in conversations later, they were not connected, as he would ask, with any circumstance or particular thought that would make me want to do that. Feeling inwardly betrayed, I believed that he was causing it in fact and treating me like I alone was responsible. In the army, I would later be shocked to discover I had undifferentiated schizophrenia, but I would not discover this until I was at Fort Jackson, South Carolina.

For the following two months in the apartment, the stress continued, and my landlord approached me on the same issue of not being connected with the fellowship, just as my previous roommates had done. He said that the guys had talked to him and had said that I was distant. He said that it was uncomfortable for them to be around me, and because of this, I was not contributing to the fellowship. He told me that it was probably time for me to move on to another apartment. I asked for forgiveness because I didn't know what else to do, and we began to meet. I also met with the other guys in my new apartment and told them "my story" as I understood it at the time and why I was so disconnected and apparently rude toward them.

That extended my time there, and they never really had to ask me to finally leave because I would soon enlist in the army as a desperate attempt to run away from all of these difficult and confusing problems, or people, or whatever it could be. I felt that it was my moral obligation to resist their efforts at ruining me, but the overriding emotion that I felt was simple yet desperate bewilderment.

At the security company where I was still working, I began to be approached on similar terms. One of my supervisors started telling me that I needed to loosen up around the guys and not seem so uptight. The last conversation he later had with me was while he was training me on the last of my three routes that I had to learn for the security car. He began raising his voice, shouting at me in the patrol car, saying that I did not listen to him. He said that he had been with the company for a number of years and that I did not listen to his instructions when he was giving them. I was surprised by this point and argued in vain that I was listening and that he did not have any cause for his frustration. I told him that I was quitting. The following day, I went back to try to salvage the job because I felt bad. They told me that the job was over, and I had to move on to somewhere else.

The next weeks were a major disappointment. I went back in an effort to make sense out of the preceding months' struggles and called up all the people I had had problems with and my former roommates, and I told them all that had happened and apologized, explaining that I could now see that the one thing at the center of all my failure was in fact relationships. I could see that much very clearly, as I told them honestly. After all, everywhere I went, people had problems with me.

It was very, very distressing believing that the key to my problem laid in relationships with people, but the simple fact was that my perceptions of people were false. I was hearing things.

Believing with conviction that these people were out to get me and to ruin my life with failure, I had to shut up about it and apologize to them because my warped mind had no other choice. They would call me crazy if I shared what my true thoughts were. Then they would really ruin my life. They would put me in a psych ward. I would be humiliated if I were said to be mentally unstable. I knew that that was what I would be seen as if I confessed all of my beliefs and told people about my ESP. I believed all normal people had ESP but that they didn't talk about it either, so I definitely shouldn't. Those people who suffered from being controlled by others even more than me fell into "the trap" of being diagnosed as mentally ill and locked up, or prevented from working. I would never let that happen to me.

All I could do was admit that I somehow had relationship problems, which I partly believed and yet couldn't. This was the main struggle at the campus, with my roommates, my coworkers, and I told them that though I did not understand or feel like an arrogant person, that that was all I could really say was my problem—relationships and arrogance, just like they had all said.

They understandably didn't know what the real problem was, and I would never blame them for not knowing. I was hearing voices that were telling me that all these people were out to get me in such a way as to ruin my life, and I was reacting to this by staying away from them and acting in bizarre ways. At least by this time I was acting out in some bizarre ways, unlike before in the previous chapter.

The stress was incredible for me. Even when I was later told that I was schizophrenic, I was even more deeply distressed. I didn't really know even then that I was truly mentally sick or that the chemicals in my brain were out of whack or whatever they will eventually find out is actually wrong with my brain. I only interpreted "being schizophrenic" as another step in other people's plot to control me and to stop me, and it was getting worse all the time. I fully believed that brainwaves from other people were ruining me. It is amazing to me, looking back, that I could be so far gone and yet be so sane now. I owe it all to modern medicine and a simple daily pill. Honestly, if it were not for Risperidone, I would be that way now. That's the bottom line.

No one at the churches that I went to saw my problems as being due to a possible mental illness. I went to two churches before joining the army and had problems at both. One was very brief, as I'm about to mention. It is concerning to me that no one considered mental illness as a serious consideration or referred me to a psychiatrist. I probably would have been offended at the idea anyway and wouldn't have gone in for any reason just the same.

Two applications of mine were turned in at other security companies. Neither of them had any positions available. Because I had quit, I did not qualify for unemployment benefits. The situation was miserable. I still had a strong sense of personal dignity, like I was responsible for everything, and I was disgusted with myself. I felt like a failure, and I "knew" it was true with whatever knowledge I had at this time.

I considered my options and talked to my parents or whoever was available. At another time, back in 2005, I had gone to the army recruiter's office and had actually taken the ASVAB test. The incentives in the military were the most helpful. I felt that I had no other options, and so I seriously considered it. I told my parents that I was going to talk to the recruiters and that I was very certain that I wanted to do it. So I scheduled my ASVAB test and went down to take it. They set me up with the information technician's job in the reserve for an army hospital in LA. We scheduled the physical, and two weeks after the decision, it was official just like that. It's amazing how I went from desperate option to option on a dime like that.

My dad must have seen the same thing because he was concerned about all of it. He had expressed that, and he had previously also been a victim in one of my nonemotional rants as well. As I have previously mentioned, schizophrenics typically struggle with loss of affect as well as affective flattening, which can result in nonemotional anger, or in my case, arguments that I was totally starting but not at all emotional about. I had cussed my dad out on the phone previously. In my mind, it was because he had not taught me ESP sooner in my life so that I would be better at it now and able to survive.

The Army Option

He actually was kind enough to take time off at work, drive all the way out from Missouri, and drive me back to be with the family in the time leading up to the army. It's terrible what I did to him. At one point after he had arrived in California, I asked if it was okay with him that I was going into the army, and he began to say that it was all right, but he expressed disappointment that I had not taken his counsel to wait and also to talk to other people about it. I argued, because I was again insulted at people trying to control me, and I told him that I had spoken with at least five people about this and that they had all agreed. I dismissed his continued warnings like I dismissed everyone's advice, because I couldn't reconcile it with the fantasy world that was stuck in my mind.

On my way toward the fridge to get a drink, I immediately fell down screaming, "God help me," and when I saw my dad's feet approach me, I got up and backed away from him, shouting, "Get away from me!" I cussed at my dad again and said some outrageous things. All the while, I had not fallen down screaming because I really wanted to do it, as if it were a conscious choice. It completely felt like it was involuntary. I still remember the complete sudden shock of it all, and it in no way ever felt like I had done it to myself.

I was as shocked as my dad. I turned and ran out the front door, probably because I was shocked and angered at what was happening. In a subsequent talk with another individual regarding the above event, he talked about the fact that they, or his family, believe that "there is a kind of man who curses his father and does not bless his mother ... (Proverbs 30:11)" and so on as the verse goes. He was saying that my problem was a serious spiritual one and I was in rebellion. It is very frustrating to be humiliated with that kind of talk when you believe that on a deeper level it is these same people who are twisting and manipulating your body and mind to do the things that they are rebuking you for in the first place. It wasn't my fault in my twisted mind. It was "their fault."

Dad wound up saying that because of my earlier use of profanity coupled with this, he did not want me to be around the family at this time. Mom and Dad still had very young children in the home, and there was understandably no other option for them. He had come down to pick me up, already knowing from previous times that we had argued on the phone and that I had used profanity in frustration. He also knew about the "fits" in the other house. He then decided to pick me up but left me at my grandparents, whom I had lived with first when I came from Missouri.

I was sincerely shocked by all this, believe it or not. Whenever things got worse, I was always genuinely surprised by all of the events, even my own behavior and everyone's responses to me, because I did not even believe that it was really my fault in the first place. I "knew" that they knew this too in their own hearts. I wondered if they would ever show me any real compassion or if they would just keep preaching at me my faults while they threatened me in my mind and then separated themselves from me.

I know that all this sounds like I am frustrated with all these dear people in my life but far from it. All I can do is relate what I felt at the time, and that's it. I was frustrated that Dad was cutting me off for what seemed to me as less than good reasons and leaving me instead with others. I did not know that I was crazy. I had no idea that they were acting rationally, and I was reacting in my own irrationality. The world was upside down to me, and I to it.

Later on, I found out that Dad had left my stuff at my uncle's and went back home. I called later and apologized, once again, for what happened. At this point, it occurred to me that all my relationship problems were just the same here as anywhere, and if I was going to deal with relationship problems anywhere in the intervening time between now and when boot camp started, it might as well be now with Mom and Dad. We had multiple conversations in the coming months via phone and e-mail. I'm sure that it was very hard and confusing for my parents.

Some very strange things came out of my mouth of course. I always understand schizophrenic people from this perspective. They say the most outrageous things, even far stranger in more severe cases than myself, but they are always trying to reason or relate or communicate in ways that make sense to their own worlds that are fully operational in their own minds. It is simply the way that they are relating to society.

Association with rebellious people comes somewhat naturally to me as well, in that I know what it is like when you can't help but wind up in arguments with well-intentioned people. And in a twisted sense, I was rebellious. People seem to think that a forceful conversation will do the trick. What winds up happening is that it spirals downward into a heated argument where both of us are totally offended at each other. Well-intentioned people don't always see that listening more than talking and responding with calmness is the best way to handle rebellion, but I digress.

I went back and forth with my parents. They kept talking. At one point, I drove out to Missouri on Christmas Day and arrived the next day. I stayed maybe a couple days and drove back. It was awful for all of us. We don't need to go into details.

At one point, my grandmother met with me, saying that they had agreed that there might be something physically wrong with me, like Tourette's syndrome, and they suggested that I go in for a physical because she had noticed ticks.

On Sunday, March 15, I arrived at a local church in Lancaster for the first service and afterwards was approached by an under shepherd, who had previously met with me, and one of the elders of the church. They talked with me about my behavior and how distanced it was. They went through the fact that I tended to come and go without any explanation. Our few counseling meetings continued.

I finished my relationship after this. They asked that I no longer attend the church. Their reason was that I should leave the church for not finishing my counseling assignments that he had been giving me. Months later, I went to boot camp, where I loved it and pretty much thrived because absolutely no one cared about me or how distanced I was. Sometimes I was strange, but because I wasn't being told to leave anywhere or being talked to about my work habits, I actually did well. I just kept my distance from everyone, and they left me alone.

Boot camp ended, and I graduated. I spent the following months at Fort Gordon working on being an IT specialist. However, there were several moments that brought back memories of employers when I got two FTRs (Failure to Report) and one insubordination.

The following failure academically in AIT school made me feel that for whatever reason I was apparently too dumb to pass the exams. The main reason was really because I was talking to people in my head. I also had a lot of strange and hurtful arguments with my parents that wouldn't be appropriate for me to bring up again. I have a great many regrets from that time that I wish had never happened. You would think that looking back on regrets that were there because of a mental illness would make it so much easier to bear, but for whatever reason, it was still very hard to deal with some of the things that I had said and done for some time afterwards.

Among the crazy things that yours truly did, I found on Facebook and proposed to a girl that I barely had known from the recent past. I argued with people too. I started trying to talk with my parents' pastor, who was the exception to the rule that everyone in my life was being rational, and he wasted no time, in the first five minutes interrupting me and saying, "You're a dead man going to hell ..." That was it! We couldn't even have a conversation. In later phone calls, it got better, and I was as gracious in my voice as possible in saying that I really didn't want to argue with him, "just express concern at the way that everyone was communicating with me." Even in my confused state, I was trying my hand at graciously handling all of these "difficult people." He told me that he thought that all the bad things in my own actions must be demons and that he would send me a book about demonology.

I went home on leave at one point, and somehow they, my parents' two pastors, had gotten it into their heads that I had fornicated. I, to this day, don't know how they got this idea. So they followed up, asking whether I had fornicated, to which I responded, "No, I've never done that!" One of them asked, "Who's the woman?" several times and lightly pounded his fist on the table very seriously and insistently. I said, "No, I'm a virgin!" laughing at them as hysterically as I could manage. They sat there and stared as if I was still showing grave disrespect at these serious questions. They probably really believed that I was for sure demonic in some way by this point, if not before. These guys were, again, the only irrational people in my story apart from myself unfortunately, not that I bear them any ill will.

Speaking about Delusions for the First Time

After I returned to Fort Jackson, I finally voiced out loud, for everyone to know, my delusions. By now, I had eventually come to believe that I really had a case of "anencephaly," that is the absence of the brain, because voices were telling me so. I told the sergeant that I was going to die because I had anencephaly, and they soon took me to the psych ward on base. That was the first time I had openly voiced something that was being told to me in my head. I had never voiced my delusions outwardly before that time.

It was awful. I still hadn't figured out that the voices were not really there. They put me on 4 mg of Risperidone. We spent the days having meetings with psychologists and a chaplain once a week and watching movies at a certain time each day. I had conversations with my family back home and would later learn that they had been relieved to hear that I was diagnosed with schizophrenia. I can imagine that they felt some serious relief, to put it mildly, at this news.

I didn't figure out that the voices were false until a couple months later after I was out of the psych ward. It suddenly dawned on me that it was all false. But I came in and out of this understanding in my first year of being medicated, and usually it was directly connected to taking or not taking my medication.

Adam W. Lambdin

My Denouement of Delusion

However, I was schizophrenic, and that was essentially uncovering all of my bad behavior and attitudes that were so far expressed. I had a sinful heart and a broken mind, and both were necessary to get me to act out as I did, at least in the actually sinful ways that I did. I understood what was wrong, and I changed relatively easily after I was medicated and in and out of counseling with a psychologist a couple of times. After that, repentance wasn't super hard regarding a number of previous concerns that people had had for me. It just came along with my sanity as I grew more rational over time, and it did take some time, but it felt so easy to change. My insanity had simply uncovered my sin hidden in my heart, which became so easy to conceal again, unfortunately in another sense. Although, I do feel that there was genuine repentance on some level all the while.

Apart from behavior, I did struggle a lot at first. I thought about death a lot. There were times when that was all I thought about. I thought about being isolated and alone in life. I felt as though I were trapped in my own skull and isolated from a world filled with normal people. That feeling of being trapped inside my skull was very real at times and intense. It made me want to scream, but I couldn't, knowing that it would only make me feel worse.

After arriving home, I would check myself into a psych ward a couple months later in Columbia, Missouri, at the VA hospital there. I struggled so hard to want to take my meds. There were days when I purposely didn't. I imagined myself coming off of them one day when I "got better." I imagined that all I needed was more self-control, and I could muscle my way out of being dependent on medication. After all, I had a less severe case.

Even in the following years, I lowered my dosage, with my psychiatrist's permission, to 3 mg. daily. This would lead to my generally taking things much more personally. When people at the dinner table would take bites of food at the same time as I did, I was offended and thought that it meant something insulting. I took the timing of words spoken personally. I took everything more personally. I kept it inside most often, but there were times of discussion with my parents that led to my own frustration and embarrassment. Eventually, I figured out that I simply needed 4 mg of Risperdal daily, and that was it.

This isn't one of those books about schizophrenics where he or she starts ranting about all the amazing lessons or his or her inspiring story or talent for insight due to incredible irrationality, as if such a thing were possible, as I have read from other people who were schizophrenic. I have read a little from one such book and was horrified and felt such pity for him because he obviously was still schizophrenic. This is just about relating to schizophrenics, their families, and their counselors. As I see it, I have no real amazing or inspiring story. It was very painful and real, and I never want to go back.

PART 3

The Ins and Outs of Schizophrenia and Its treatment

CHAPTER 4

The Biological Basis of Schizophrenia

This is the chapter where I go into great pains to explain the science of schizophrenia, not that I understand it incredibly well myself. This is the only chapter that is hard to understand. I apologize for that. I originally did this research for a graduate-level class, and I struggle to find simple ways to explain the medical nature of schizophrenia without using big words and scientific jargon. I ask that you push through this chapter even if you struggle to understand, but this is the only chapter that is like this.

Schizophrenia is a very devastating illness that is characterized by hallucinations, or hearing things, and it frequently occurs with delusions, believing things that aren't true, that can be grandiose or negative in nature. It is accompanied by loss of familial, professional, and otherwise personal social functioning. Sufferers also experience emotional impairment and emotional pain involving depression or anxiety. They can also suffer with a loss of affect, which is the loss of ability to feel or to express emotion. The medical causes of schizophrenia, or its etiology, is unknown. It is reasonable to presume that it originates in biological causes or dispositions because of a myriad of medical data, not to mention the fact that counseling, while certainly a help with cases after medication, is not an actual cure, as is demonstrated by the fact that schizophrenics by and large remain schizophrenics even after counseling.

Adam W. Lambdin

According to the website, UpToDate.Com, which is based on the most current medical information, which doctors use as a reference, is the following:

> Schizophrenia is a psychiatric disorder involving chronic or recurrent psychosis. It is commonly associated with impairments in social and occupational functioning. It is among the most disabling and economically catastrophic medical disorders, ranked by the World Health Organization as one of the top ten illnesses contributing to the global burden of disease. Characteristics of Schizophrenia typically include positive symptoms such as hallucinations or delusions, disorganized speech, negative symptoms such as a flat affect or poverty of speech, and impairments in cognition including attention, memory and executive functions. A diagnosis of Schizophrenia is based on the presence of such symptoms, coupled with social or occupational dysfunction for at least six months in the absence of another diagnoses that would better account for the presentation.[2]

There are a lot of things to address in the beliefs that secular psychiatrists and biblical counselors each bring to the table. Psychiatrists assume that all things are caused by chemicals and that there is no soul, just whatever is caused as a result of neurons firing in the brain. Biblical counselors assume that a soul exists and can think absent the body (i.e., at death). They presuppose that the soul is in charge of the body and cooperates with it. Both of these come into play in

---

[2] Richard Hermann, "Schizophrenia: Clinical Manifestations, Course, Assessment, and Diagnosis," UpToDate.Com, July 26, 2013, accessed February 24, 2015, http://www.uptodate.com/contents/schizophrenia-clinical-manifestations-course-assessment-and-diagnosis.

their respective theories of the origins of schizophrenia and of mental illnesses in general.

Biblical counselors have traditionally believed that sin has some part to play in the cause, or at least influences the problem as the body and the soul interact. They may assert that the problem is a hybrid between the soul and the body. Psychiatrists, on the other hand, presume that mental illness is no more than a mis-functioning brain. I can see either point.

Mental illness and schizophrenia have a long history. The *Comprehensive Textbook of Psychiatry VI* says, "Greek physicians described the deterioration in cognitive functions and personality commonly observed in schizophrenic patients today."[3] Then, later, the Dark Ages brought in superstition and thus a recession in the progress made in the overall understanding of this illness. "Schizophrenia did not reemerge as a medical condition worthy of study and treatment until the 18th century."[4]

As time went on, medicine attempted to differentiate the various classifications of insanity. A hindrance to this development was the ability to distinguish between bipolar and schizophrenia because of general paresis, which *Dorland's Medical Dictionary* defines as "A brain disease occurring as a late consequence of syphilis."[5] "The cause of this syphilitic insanity was subsequently traced to a spirochetal or a type of bacterial infection, and antibiotics were eventually found to be effective in treatment and prevention."[6] Later on, Kraepelin would distinguish between dementia precox (dementia of the young), which

---

[3] William T. Carpenter and Robert W. Buchanan, *Comprehensive Textbook of Psychiatry VI*, edited by Harold I. Kaplan and Benjamin J. Sadock (Baltimore, MD: Williams and Wilkins, 1995), 889.
[4] Ibid.
[5] *Dorland's Medical Dictionary for Health Consumers*, S.v. "paresis," retrieved April 3 2015 from http://medical-dictionary.thefreedictionary.com/paresis.
[6] William T. Carpenter and Robert W. Buchanan, *Comprehensive Textbook of Psychiatry VI*, edited by Harold I. Kaplan and Benjamin J. Sadock (Baltimore, MD: Williams and Wilkins, 1995), 889.

had a poor long-term prognosis, with manic-depressive illness, which had a better long-term prognosis.[7]

Kraepelin also formed the foundation for the current understanding of both *positive symptoms* of schizophrenia, which are the thoughts, behaviors, or sensory perceptions that are characteristic of a person with schizophrenia, and *negative symptoms*, which are affective flattening (lack of emotion or expression) or impoverishment of that person's speech.

In 1911, Eugen Bleuler observed that actual dementia was not really characteristic of dementia precox. He dubbed this disease "schizophrenia," which means a "splitting of the mind." The Kaplan and Sadock *Comprehensive Textbook of Psychiatry VI*, which I will continue to reference throughout this chapter, goes on to say:

> Bleuler introduced the concept of primary and secondary schizophrenic symptoms; his four primary symptoms (the four A's) were abnormal associations, autistic behavior and thinking, abnormal affect, and ambivalence. Of those four symptoms Bleuler viewed as central to the illness the loss of association between thought processes and among thought, emotion, and behavior. Typical examples of the loss of association are silly giggling on receiving news of the death of a loved one, the introduction of magical thinking and peculiar concepts into an ordinary discussion, the sudden display of angry behavior without experiencing anger (or an understandable provocation), and the like.[8]

Blueler's view was that schizophrenia is a single disease entity that causes a dissociative process that undergirds a wide variety of symptoms. There are parallels in disease for this concept:

---

[7] Ibid.
[8] Ibid.

Diabetic patients have in common an impairment in glucose metabolism, but the secondary manifestations vary considerably, depending on which organ systems are involved. Similarly, seizure disorders may share a common pathophysiological mechanism, but the location of the lesion leads to different signs and symptoms.

Likewise, there are a wide variety of manifestations of syphilitic insanity. Therefore, there is some basis for a single disease understanding of schizophrenia. However, the Kaplan and Sadock textbook chooses to define schizophrenia as a syndrome for the time being because there is a lack of evidence for a single disease.

Thomas Szasz

Some individuals have chosen to define schizophrenia as a "sane reaction to an insane world," or the "societal reaction theory." On really the same level of believability, Thomas Szasz proposed the theory that mental illnesses were merely society's myth. He believed that a mental illness was merely the culture's inappropriate way of managing wrong or evil behavior. Szasz wrote in an article published in the *Journal of Biblical Counseling*, volume 14, number 1, in the fall of 1995:

> ... (some so-called) psychotics assert that they hear voices that command them to kill their wives or children; psychiatrists assert that such persons suffer from a brain disease called "schizophrenia," which can be effectively treated with certain chemicals; and I claim that the assertions of psychotics and psychiatrists alike are claims unsubstantiated by evidence. The point, however, is that psychiatrists have the power to accredit their own claims as scientific facts and rational treatments, discredit the claims of

mental patients and psychiatric critics as delusions and denials, and enlist the coercive power of the state to impose their views on involuntary "patients."[9]

Szasz's article above is entitled "Mental Illness Is Still a Myth." There is no mistaking it. He repeatedly appeals to the apparent tolerance of evil acts in our judicial system due to a diagnosis of "mentally ill." He really seems to conjure up a lot of bitter sentiment to his cause in this regard. His passion to prove that mental illness is a myth is clearly false, however. Most mentally ill persons are harmless anyway.

In the article, he admits to going to school to become a licensed psychiatrist merely to prove that mental illnesses are fundamentally false ideas. However, playing on people's suspicion of injustice as the main argument for the illegitimacy of schizophrenia as a disease is not the way to go about it in the first place. The Kaplan and Sadock volumes of *Comprehensive Textbook of Psychiatry VI* were published the same year that Szasz wrote for the *Journal of Biblical Counseling* in 1995, which makes this interesting from that standpoint because of the medical knowledge available at the time.

The Evidence

Schizophrenia manifests itself in all societies and locations of the world. Psychosis in men tends to onset in the ages of fifteen to twenty-five years of age. Women's onset occurs in the ages of twenty-five to thirty-five years of age.[10] This brings up a very interesting point on the issue of whether or not this is a biological or organic illness, as persons in the biblical counseling community so often question. If a person is

---

[9] Thomas Szasz, "Mental Illness Is Still a Myth," *Journal of Biblical Counseling* 14, no. 1 (fall 1995): 37.
[10] William T. Carpenter and Robert W. Buchanan, *Comprehensive Textbook of Psychiatry VI*, edited by Harold I. Kaplan and Benjamin J. Sadock (Baltimore, MD: Williams and Wilkins, 1995), 890.

going to assert that schizophrenia is not, at least somehow, rooted in biology, then that person has to explain why its onset is so predictable in this way, one for men, and another for women. A person would expect this illness, if it were not rooted in biology, to manifest itself in a far less predictable manner, but it does not.

Doctors have wrestled with the issue of whether schizophrenia is due to a neurodevelopmental problem or a neuropathological problem. In other words, they have wrestled with whether it is due, in the first case, to a failure of the brain to develop properly, or whether it is due to a disease process that alters a normal brain. Both of these are possibilities in the presumption that the illness is a syndrome. According to the Kaplan and Sadock textbook, some random occasions of gliosis appear in schizophrenic brains. MedicineNet.Com defines Gliosis as:

> A process leading to scars in the central nervous system that involves the production of a dense fibrous network of neuroglia (supporting cells) in areas of damage. Gliosis is a prominent feature of many diseases of the central nervous system, including multiple sclerosis and stroke. After a stroke, neurons die and disappear with replacement Gliosis.[11]

This indicates a potential disease process and thus a "subsequent neuropathological response,"[12] but the mass of evidence regarding the onset of deviations in the development of the brain point more consistently to a neurodevelopmental problem.

This leads to another major point as to the biological nature of schizophrenia:

---

[11] MedicineNet.Com, "Definition of Gliosis," last modified June 14, 2012, accessed April 2, 2015, http://www.medicinenet.com/script/main/art.asp?articlekey=25457

[12] William T. Carpenter and Robert W. Buchanan, *Comprehensive Textbook of Psychiatry VI*, edited by Harold I. Kaplan and Benjamin J. Sadock (Baltimore, MD: Williams and Wilkins, 1995), 891.

> Schizophrenia and schizophrenialike manifestations occur at an increased rate among the biological relatives of patients with schizophrenia. The increased rate is most evident in the case of monozygotic twins, who have an identical genetic endowment and a concordance rate for schizophrenia between 40 and 50 percent. That rate is four to five times the concordance rate in dizygotic twins or the rate of occurrence in other first-degree relatives (siblings, parents, or offspring). The finding of a higher rate of Schizophrenia among the biological relatives of an adopted-away person who develops schizophrenia than among adoptive, nonbiological relatives who rear the patient has added further support to pedigree and twin study evidence suggesting a significant genetic contribution to the etiology of schizophrenia. However, the modes of genetic transmission in schizophrenia are unknown.[13]

The authors go on to say on the same page that just because some persons exhibit a genetic vulnerability for schizophrenia does not mean that they will get it. It is postulated that there must be environmental influence that may either prevent or cause the illness in such a genetically vulnerable individual. However, figuring out exactly what is the "mode of transmission" is not possible until there is a phenotype or an observable interaction of the genotype with the environment.[14]

There are a number of other hypotheses and theories about the etiology of schizophrenia. The diagnosis of schizophrenia remains clinical. It cannot be done through PEG, CT, or MRI scans, for example. However, scans have brought to light a variety of differences in a schizophrenic brain as opposed to a normal brain. These do remain varied and inconsistent, but it is common.

---

[13] Ibid.
[14] Ibid.

Doctors have found that schizophrenics can have all kinds of differences with their brain structure. They can oftentimes have, for example, "enlargement of the cortical sulci and lateral and third ventricles, overall reduction in gray matter and whole brain volume, diminution in size of temporal lobe structures, thinning of the cerebellar folia, alterations in corpus callosum size and shape, changes in cerebral asymmetry, and altered brain density."[15]

It consists of things that do not always occur in only a schizophrenic brain. It is common for psychiatrists to call the cause of schizophrenia a "chemical imbalance" because it is comforting to the one suffering with schizophrenia and is not altogether untrue if you refer to the above as a "chemical imbalance." However, this specific type of etiology is not a confirmed fact if you define it in narrower terms.

The Biblical Counseling Community

In his book *Blame It on the Brain,* Edward T. Welch asserts:

> Most psychiatric problems are hybrids—a combination of spiritual problems and physical ones. For example, while the hallucinations of schizophrenia may be physical, the guilt that is part of almost all schizophrenia is clearly spiritual. In these cases, not only will Scripture teach people how to live godly lives in the midst of possible ongoing hallucinations, it will deal directly with a person's guilt. And there will be some cases of schizophrenia where guilt is actually the cause of the physical symptoms.[16]

---

[15] Karen Berman, David Daniel, and Daniel Weinberger, *Comprehensive Textbook of Psychiatry VI*, edited by Harold I. Kaplan and Benjamin J. Sadock (Baltimore, MD: Williams and Wilkins, 1995), 915.

[16] Edward T. Welch, *Blame It on the Brain* (Phillisburg, New Jersey: P and R Publishing, 1998), 107.

But the guilt that a schizophrenic person experiences could itself be delusional. Speaking as a Schizophrenic person myself, I am not in complete disagreement with what Welch has said here (understood rightly) and especially with what Charles Hodges said in his lecture called "Schizophrenia" at the 2014 Association of Certified Biblical Counselors conference in Sun Valley, California.

It is difficult to say that the spiritual problems in a schizophrenic person are not simply emerging because that person cannot distinguish between the real world and his delusions. A sinful heart yields sin, but delusions can reveal what is in the heart because there is no holding back like the rest of us do when we are perfectly sane. I believe that sin is revealed in a schizophrenic person more readily than the average person. If they struggle with guilt, for example, it is quite possibly in part because they are believing things that aren't true. Take away the delusions, and you have a "normal" person. It's not complicated. Should we presume that sinful guilt is making a number of schizophrenic persons what they are? No.

Charles Hodges's lecture at the ACBC conference was straightforward. He says, "This is a disease, and it does not have the kind of course we would expect with most. Most diseases that we see are [solvable by listening to your doctor] ..."[17] but he says that schizophrenia is not this way at all. Also, 80 percent of the people that get off their medication will relapse or get worse. He says also that people who recover, he would say, never had schizophrenia in the first place. The bottom line is that Hodges says that schizophrenia is in fact a "disease." He talks about it like it is a medical problem. He says, "It has an underlying cause."[18] He talks about the promising theories and studies regarding the cause or causes of schizophrenia. He also believes that schizophrenia has actual pathology. Jay Adams and Thomas Szasz in 1995 in the *Journal of Biblical Counseling* never would have said this. This indicates to me that

---

[17] Charles Hodges, *Schizophrenia* (The Association of Certified Biblical Counselors Annual Conference, 2014).
[18] Ibid.

there has been great change in the biblical counseling movement that no one is really talking about specifically, at least in the case of Hodges. I could be wrong, but that is what seems to be true.

This lecture is, however, a great resource for biblical counselors who have read and are confused by previous voices in the biblical counseling movement. I myself had to read, for my graduate-level biblical counseling class, Thomas Szasz's article from the *Journal of Biblical Counseling*, quoted above, as well as Jay Adams's article claiming that schizophrenia was chiefly caused by an accumulation of sins against the body. Both of these were assigned to me in my Counseling and Physiology class for the MA in biblical counseling program.

Charles Hodges's lecture is the only reason that I think that there has been really solid change. I believe that Jay Adams's assessment of schizophrenia was horrendous. Thomas Szasz was horrendous. Ed Welch said that schizophrenia is a hybrid of spiritual and physical problems, which is better but requires more understanding when applied in actual counseling. He wrote that some time ago actually. I would be interested in what he thinks now. In the first place, the spiritual problems should be distinguished from the schizophrenia itself, and that statement in the chapter by Welch would again require a lot more explanation. On the other hand, Charles Hodges theorizes that schizophrenia is "An autoimmune disorder which is ravaging parts of that person's brain which accounts for the progressive nature of the problem,"[19] in his lecture. He never even suggests that sin is the problem at all. He does say that if a person recovers, they probably never had it, but the differences in thinking between Charles Hodges and the rest of the biblical counselors that I mentioned and quoted is stark.

For example, a dissertation written by James R. Eichelberger called "A Christian Counselor's Experience in Working with Schizophrenics in the State Hospital System and Preliminary Treatment Suggestions" blatantly calls biblical counselors to confront delusions as sin. He does ironically acknowledge that he saw little to no results from his efforts,

---

[19] Ibid.

but he was working based on assumptions that were false. Of course this was in 1987 and far from the current level of understanding that Charles Hodges represents in our movement now. My point is that he represents the traditional mishaps in biblical counseling.

Sin and Schizophrenia

It is not true that schizophrenia is driven by spiritual problems. A counselor should never assume that sin is the cause of "schizophrenia" unless the counselee comes to see this him or herself and is in full remission. In other words, he or she is of sound mind and, according to Hodges would have never even had schizophrenia, in his opinion. A counselor should only allow this to be discovered as the counselee is guided to this herself or himself along the way. Even if sin is identified as a cause of some problems, that does not dispense with the idea that this person is somehow genetically predisposed to this weakness, which requires additional understanding. We really do not understand all the intricacies of an incredibly complex spiritual and physical mechanism. A counselor will just never know all that is involved, and no one knows the heart. Paul said he could not even judge himself.

However, sin can still be dealt with as it comes up without feeling the need to establish that it is in fact "the root problem" or "the actual cause." Sin can be dealt with in its own right without attacking the nature of its being there. A person can deal with it for what it is. And the guilt that Welch says is rampant in schizophrenics can very often be a mere part of their delusions, or maybe they are guilty because they are delusional. That would need to be dealt with by a biblical counselor. Of course, guilt is deep within all people's hearts, and even schizophrenics should otherwise deal with it biblically.

Oftentimes, I wondered in the past in regards to my own case, *What came first? The sinful stuff, like fear or depression, or the irrationality that seemed to cause them? How much of which was biological?* I wondered whether my delusions were in fact sinful themselves. I think that I was confused because of thinking from biblical counselors of the past, but Charles Hodges seemed to be much more accurate with regard to his overall approach to this illness, which was very comforting when I heard it because I sympathized with ACBC.

Other Causes

But schizophrenia is not totally and only caused by biological factors alone. A book called *Origins and Development of Schizophrenia*, edited by Lenzenweger and Dworkin, which I found on the American Psychological Association's website, refers to a study on page 9 that says the following:

> Data on gene-environment interactions in schizophrenia have been provided from studies of African Caribbean individuals who immigrated to the United Kingdom. Sugerman and Craufurd (1994) found that the parents of African Caribbean and White schizophrenia patients had approximately similarly increased risks for developing the disorder (i.e., genetic predisposition is an important risk factor for schizophrenia in the African Caribbean community); however, the siblings of second-generation African Caribbean probands who were born in the United Kindgom were at significantly greater risk than any other relative group (i.e., environmental risk factors more common in the African Caribbean immigrant community were operative).[20]

The point is that the environment or the difficulties of cultural assimilation and adjustments that the children of the immigrants to

---

[20] Tyrone D. Cannon, *Origins and Development of Schizophrenia*, edited by Mark F. Lenzwenweger and Robert H. Dworkin (Washington, DC: American Psychological Association, 1998), 9.

the UK had to face had a factor in increasing the risk for their becoming schizophrenic, while their parents who had been born and raised in their homeland maintained the same risk factors as native persons do elsewhere.

How do we understand genetic and environmental factors, both of which increase the risk for schizophrenia? And if the stressors of cultural assimilation, for example, increase the risk for becoming schizophrenic, how can we assert that sin is causing it in such a case? Is it sinful responses that cause the disease or is it the stressors themselves? Apparently, just being stressed by life adjustments can be a contributing factor, but that wouldn't be sin per se. Sin would be how a person responds to stressful situations, which might not even matter.

The same book goes on to argue in chapter 3 for the correspondence of obstetric (birth) complications such as hypoxia (lack of oxygen) and the occurrence of schizophrenia in such persons later on. It says on page 69 that 20–30 percent of schizophrenics experienced hypoxia (lack of oxygen) related problems at or before birth.[21] I find that fascinating because at my own birth, my mother's placenta began to calcify up to several days before my birth, which I presume could have contributed in a similar way to my own development of schizophrenia in my early twenties.

None of this cancels out the need to deal with sin and guilt, as Edward Welch pointed out in his book, *Blame It on the Brain*, but it calls into question the need that many biblical counselors have felt to get such a person to the point where they no longer need their medication as much or at all, as one such biblical counselor with whom I spoke briefly admitted to me on the phone. Not all biblical counselors see these issues the same way at all. They differ drastically between more of a Jay Adams/Thomas Szasz approach or a more Charles Hodges kind of approach, if I were to judge so from my own experiences.

---

[21] Tyrone D. Cannon, *Origins and Development of Schizophrenia*, edited by Mark F. Lenzwenweger and Robert H. Dworkin (Washington, DC: American Psychological Association, 1998), 9.

Biblical counselors should basically agree with psychiatrists about schizophrenia based on what Hodges has confirmed. Schizophrenia is a disease that has pathology, again according to Hodges. It also results in diverse physical changes to the brain itself. It comes at a specific time in people's lives, one for men and another for women. The rate of concordance for monozygotic twins is 40–50 percent. It still occurs more often in persons within the same biological family even if they were adopted into another family. It can be brought out in a given population by environmental stressors or emigration (in the earlier above). It seems that while psychiatrists do not yet know the specific etiology of schizophrenia, they do know that it is very much biological in nature, whatever other questions we might ask in the nature-versus-nurture aspect.

CHAPTER 5
Therapy Versus Soul Care

An integrationist wants to work Christianity into the mold of the psychological system. He or she takes a psychological system of choice and mixes in some Christian concepts. The result is a method that is secular psychology that uses Christian words to whatever degree. Biblical counselors have fought hard to make sure that the Bible is the only tool we use. However, I ask, can we make use of psychology and still be pleasing God as Christian counselors? I think that we can even though fundamentally the Bible and psychology offer different answers to our problems, and you have to choose between one and the other. Psychology and the Bible are like two separate categories on a Venn diagram with a central area where the circles overlap, and the two groups can actually harmonize in the central area of common sense. I believe that, as a consequence, biblical counselors can borrow from psychology when it comes to therapy for certain mentally ill persons, because it is just a kind of common sense. There are certain treatments that psychotherapists offer that make sense, but I say that the proof is in the pudding.

I myself, being diagnosed with undifferentiated schizophrenia, for which I take 4 mg of Risperidone daily, have experienced a variety of responses firsthand. However, during my onset of acute symptoms, no one would have been able to tell that I would have eventually recovered so well. I only mention my own story in this chapter for the purpose of relating how varied people's responses were to my own condition both before and after diagnosis.

For example, a biblical counselor believed both before and after my official diagnosis in the army that I had essentially relationship problems that needed to be addressed biblically. He told me after my diagnosis while in the army, "If you deal with your relationship problems, you will deal with your schizophrenia." Besides that, my parents' pastor, before I was diagnosed, sent me a book entitled *Demonology*. He then argued with me repeatedly both before and after diagnosis about my need to get saved and to repent. After my medical discharge from the army, he told me that my problem must have been "demons whispering in my ears." The psychiatrists and psychologists at Veteran's Affairs treated me as a patient and helped me, either through medication or some brief occasions of counseling that I went in for, in order to become more rational. Likewise, I believe that the relationship that I developed with my local pastor was therapeutic in regards to my fears, anxieties, and depression that followed for some time after my medical discharge. All that to say, many people treated me very differently, and there was certainly some degree of differences among the various reactions to my condition.

Schizophrenia is diabolical because it is characterized by confusion of the psyche—that is, delusions and hallucinations. The soul is what guides and directs the body. If the soul were confused and that was it, then biblical soul care could step in and be a real solution for schizophrenia, but that is not it. The body and the soul interact. It is true that the soul can think without the body (i.e., after death), but while encased in this body, it is limited. For example, the body dictates when a person sleeps, eats, and it otherwise influences thought via chemicals firing between neural synapses. It is true that the soul makes the decision on when specifically to eat and sleep, but to a very definite degree, the body needs these things when it needs it. All that to say that a physical brain limits a soul in a very natural way, and a damaged brain causes confusion and duress of the soul. It's logical. Therefore, this fallen body limits the soul in very practical ways, and all that means that schizophrenia is not principally a problem of the soul. It is a biological trait and/or disposition that can be managed and improved through medication and counseling.

The Approach

It is important that there be a characteristic assumption on the part of the counselor that there is as much struggle of the mind rooted in biological issues as is practical. The only reason it is important to say this is that there are a lot of assumptions to the contrary on the part of many biblical counselors, and in all fairness, sin definitely needs to be dealt with in every case.

However, there is a major difference between the counselor who asks, "Would you be willing to consider the prospect of sin in your life as well?" and the counselor who states that he or she is not there for medical treatment. "I am only concerned with confronting the sin in your life," as if that were all up front and in your face that mattered. The point is that the first question does not assume sin is the cause because the brain and the soul interact in ways no one fully understands. The biblical counselor should never assume that sin is at the root of any problem when dealing with a legitimate mental illness. She or he should assume the best about this individual and come alongside in a supportive manner, not in such a way as to "hammer down on these apparent sin issues."

The point is that while damage by external or internal means can alter the way that a person's brain operates, both secular and biblical counseling have been known to help persons who suffer with this illness. That gets back to the principle that while the body can be the cause of delusions and hallucinations, a person can trigger this disposition both initially, due to stress or life-altering events, as well as later in such a way that can cause delusions and hallucinations to only get worse, or at the very least, not get better as time advances.

The person, or their soul, can respond negatively or positively, but this is not to say that physicians know the mode of transmission of this illness, or how they become schizophrenic, in genetically vulnerable persons. They do not at this point. However, it does not mean that counseling cannot be a great help either to simply *transcend* the circumstance spiritually in some practical way or to possibly prevent it from getting worse or to improve it in regards to behavioral issues.

However, the advance of time has demonstrated that treating schizophrenics as though they were sinfully erring in their delusions and calling them to repentance is not an appropriate means of counsel. Some biblical counselors seem to think this even now, in spite of the recent conference at Grace Community Church on the subject in 2014. At the same time, a person should not preclude the remote possibility that a person may in fact be needful of spiritual correction in this regard because she or he is "faking it," just like David did toward the Philistines for fear of his life, but this is obviously not typical by far, despite the few related examples touted in times past.

I am sure that a number of persons suffering have been greatly motivated to come off of their medication after reading Jay Adams's article on the subject with accounts of miraculously cured individuals in response to his own counsel. Long-term accounts of these people after their initial counseling are not included by Adams though, to my knowledge, and Charles Hodges would say that persons who do manage to recover simply never had the disease. Needless to say, after I personally decided to come off of my medication, due to Adams's article, which is now over forty years old, I began to subside into delusions again. I was not the same person without daily doses of Risperidone, and after some degree of drama, I was convinced to get back on the meds.

The Tension between the Biblical Counselor and the Secular

Biblical counseling aside, what is interesting about secular psychotherapy for schizophrenia is how practical it really is. It is based on how to make a schizophrenic person think more rationally, although it is very often not possible to do this without quieting the voices in a given individual's mind by taking medication. Many schizophrenics will complain about not even being able to listen to a counselor because their auditory hallucinations (hearing things or voices) are "so loud" that they simply can't hear. The first thing to do is to lower or eliminate these auditory hallucinations with medication, which works most but certainly not all of the time.

As a side note, it is interesting that biblical counselors tend to repeatedly say that medication works "often," but they shy away from "most" of the time, as secular sources and Christian integrationists seem to say. This would be an interesting subject to delve into to see exactly what causes one or the other to use either term "most" or "often." I do know that biblical counselors seem to quote often only the dissenting voices in the medical community.

All this aside, it appears that psychologists and psychiatrists are not totally given to medications as the only way to eliminate the symptoms in a schizophrenic. They believe in counseling and in family therapy, as well as the value of spiritual guidance, should the individual be so inclined to receive it. My own psychiatrist, for example, has specifically acknowledged the therapeutic nature of pastoral care. However, not just from my own subjective experience, it is apparent that there are many psychologists and psychiatrists who are aware of the need to counsel and of some of the limitations of medications and so forth.

The biblical counseling movement seems to not see the need for a psychologist even in the case of a truly mentally ill person, such as a schizophrenic. Training in ACBC itself seeks to offer biblical or spiritual solutions for how to provide therapy for a schizophrenic person, which is not necessarily a bad thing at face value. I myself am afraid that there are, however, a number of ACBC certified counselors out there who are likely to harbor the belief that schizophrenic persons preferably need to get to the place where medication is no longer necessary or at least less so, though they would never say so to the counselee. They simply expect that the counselee will naturally get to that point. They might believe that *willful sin* or *concealed sin* is still frequently, at the very least, contributing to a schizophrenic's symptoms. This is not necessarily the case. It would make sense given the history of Jay Adams's

Adam W. Lambdin

opinions from long before the contemporary, current level of medical understanding concerning this illness within the ACBC community.

It is true that a schizophrenic person is still sinful, and just like all diseases of the mind, schizophrenia uncovers a deeper-rooted sinfulness that a sane individual manages to keep concealed. However, delusions and hallucinations are not sins in themselves. A "broken mind" is no more sinful than a broken leg in fact. Perhaps what "the voices" are saying to an individual is from out of a sinful heart, and perhaps the grandiose thoughts that a schizophrenic person believes about himself or herself uncover a sinful nature deep within. However, that is not *innately* worse than the average imaginations that every individual person entertains on a daily basis.

Understanding this reveals that it is totally appropriate to kindly reprove a schizophrenic's irrationality first of all and then perhaps his or her sin in the right situation. However, just as if to confront a person's delusions or hallucinations assuming that they were sinful should be no more "profound," in essence, a rebuke than if it were a confrontation of the average person's typical vainglorious thoughts and simple misconceptions of people. To confront and deny irrationality is foremost in the mind of therapy, in this instance. However, biblical counselors are not, from a practical standpoint, trained to do therapy as well as a psychologist is. That is the simple reality of the situation. Biblical counselors do soul care by definition, which I am not saying is at all a bad thing. I have been helped tremendously by my own pastor, who has no training in psychotherapy whatsoever. However, that is why a psychologist or an integrationist is sometimes or oftentimes needful, though biblical counseling can be encouraging and offer spiritual hope to her or to him at the same time as he or she is meeting with a good psychologist.

Biblical Counseling

Biblical counselors take their cue from 2 Peter 1:3 where it says that we have "everything we need for life and godliness." My case is that this does not necessarily mean that biblical counseling can cure schizophrenia or any ailment but only that it gives what is necessary to transcend circumstances with character and godliness, whatever they may be in spite of them, delusional or not.

Biblical counseling can do a great deal of good if it takes its cue from encouragement based on biblical doctrines of trust based on God's sovereignty instead of irrational fear in the schizophrenic's heart. Instead, many persons remind me of the counsel of Job's friends who told him that he is suffering because of sin. In a similar way, ACBC has traditionally taken the position (even though it appears differently today) that a person can't suffer psychologically specifically in regards to schizophrenia without sin being the cause or a cause.

Psychotherapy

The truth is that secular psychology does in fact offer practical help in confronting an individual's irrational thoughts as a schizophrenic that even ACBC could learn from in this case. For example, in the *Clinical Handbook of Psychological Disorders*, Nicolas Tarrier enumerates specific treatments for a schizophrenic person. One of many is the one called "Modified Self-Statements and Internal Dialogue." He says:

> In each case the patient is taught statements that direct the appropriate response, such as "I don't need to be afraid," "I need to keep going and get on the bus," or "Why do I think that man is looking at me when I've never seen him before?" Within the session, the patient is first asked to repeat the set of statements or questions out loud when given the appropriate cue. The verbalized statements are then gradually reduced in loudness until they are internalized. The patient then practices these in simulated situations within the session. Learning such questioning

statements is a useful stage in generating and evaluating alternative explanations for experience.[22]

Another example from the same source is "Reattribution." Tarrier writes:

> Initially, when we started coping training, we used reattributions that were illness related, such as "It's not a real voice, it's my illness," We have since abandoned this as unhelpful. We now try to use other, alternative explanations: "It may seem like a real voice, but it's just my own thoughts" and "It may seem as though people are looking at me, but they have to look somewhere."[23]

Yet another method from the same source is "Awareness Training." Tarrier writes:

> Patients not only become aware of their experiences but they also try to accept these experiences but not react to them. Patients are aware of their voices but do not react to them or become captured by their content. One function of awareness training is to make patients aware of the form and characteristics of their thoughts and perceptions rather than the content—for example, to monitor the physical onset of a voice, then use attention switching reduces the emotional impact of the content.[24]

These three examples illustrate that psychologists and, by extension, integrationists can be very practical in how they do therapy for

---

[22] Tarrier, Nicolas. 2008. *Clinical Handbook of Psychotic Disorders*. (New York City, NY: The Guilford Press), 474.
[23] Ibid.
[24] Ibid.

a schizophrenic. The first example is simply encouragement for a schizophrenic to talk to himself in a rational way, saying something like, for example, "That person is not looking at me. I've never seen that person before, and there is no reason for him to look at me." This self-talk can be very helpful if a person is disciplined and persistent. Another way to talk to oneself would be, "It may seem like a real voice, but it's just my own thoughts." Again, the author encourages a schizophrenic to switch his or her attention from the misconception to something else specific, thus minimizing the emotional impact of the original thought.

This demonstrates that a secular psychologist or integrationist would be very helpful in dealing with schizophrenia. An article written in the *Journal of Family Psychiatry* by four authors says the following:

> A growing body of research leads us to believe that strengthening family cohesion may help decrease patient psychiatric symptoms and improve quality of life for both patients and their care-givers. For example, using cross-sectional data obtained from the Family Environment Scale, Weisman, Rosales, Kymalainen, and Armesto (2005) found that greater perceived family cohesion was associated with less severe psychiatric symptoms and lower levels of depression, anxiety, and stress in schizophrenia patients.[25]

This article goes on to present a study that showed evidence for the benefits of family-based therapy. They argue that the results demonstrate that family-focused treatment yields significant results. They also say the following in the same study referencing other studies:

---

[25] Amy Weisman de Mamani et al., "A Randomized Clinical Trial to Test the Efficacy of a Family-Focused, Culturally Informed Therapy for Schizophrenia," *Journal of Family Psychology* 28, no. 6 (Dec. 2014) US: American Psychological Association: 801.

> "For example, Shah et al. (2011) found that greater self-reported spiritual connection was associated with lower negative symptoms. Mohr et al. (2011) found that patients with schizophrenia who reported using religion to help them adaptively cope with symptoms had fewer negative symptoms and reported a better quality of life 3 years later."[26]

All this indicates that psychology at large is a very helpful tool in treating mental illnesses such as schizophrenia. They acknowledge the benefits of family and religion, and their psychotherapy is practical and focuses on correcting irrationality.

All this indicates that an integrationist would probably be a good source for help in regards to schizophrenia. There may be some spiritual principles such as self-esteem that would not be the same as the biblical counsel that a certified biblical counselor would emphasize. This is where an integrationist could learn from a biblical counselor, but a biblical counselor could also learn from an integrationist in regards to practical therapy for a schizophrenic. There are practical methods for treating schizophrenia that psychology has developed due to God's common grace for humanity. At the same time, there are specific things that biblical counseling does right because it is based on the Bible, which promises that God has given us everything "sufficient for life and godliness." But the two are in harmony when both are not in contradiction to the Bible.

The Past

The previously mentioned lecture about schizophrenia by Charles Hodges was appropriate and helpful for an understanding of schizophrenia from what can be seen. He called it a "disease" that has "pathology." I repeat this example to emphasize a point. It is encouraging

---

[26] Ibid.

to hear this disease treated like what it really is, but Jay Adams gave a different depiction of it published originally in 1976. There is no need to overly criticize Jay Adams. He wrote over forty years before now, and that was long before the current level of understanding of what schizophrenia is. Unfortunately, this article was republished by the *Journal of Biblical Counseling* in 1995, and therein Adams says in this republished article entitled, "The Christian Approach to Schizophrenia":

> How does a counselor in the Christian tradition begin to handle the many problems of schizophrenic behavior? That a person experiencing such problems may be subject to (or may subject himself to) internal and external forces that may impair his ability to function, that he is capable of intentionally and unintentionally stimulating and simulating such impairment in order to mislead, and that over a period of time (or suddenly) he can develop such faulty responses to stress situations that he loses a grip on reality (i.e., he may misread it) is to picture him at once as a frail, conniving, self-deceptive, and foolish being. That is to say, as Christians look at it, the person is a sinner, who, according to the Bible, has been subjected by God to vanity because of his rebellion against his Creator.
>
> Sin, the violation of God's laws, has both direct and indirect consequences that account for all of the bizarre behavior of schizophrenics. That is why Christians must refuse to ignore the biblical data. From the perspective of these Scriptural data all faulty behavior (which for the Christian is behavior that does not conform to the law of God) stems ultimately from the fundamental impairment of each

human being at birth in consequence of the corruption of mankind resulting from the fall.[27]

Jay Adams goes on to strongly suggest that schizophrenia, excepting specific physical causes, that can be detected by medical examinations such as a tumor on an MRI is caused by sinful choices such as sleep loss, for example, that in turn eventually lead to chemical imbalances that cause hallucinations and misperceptions and thus, in a word, schizophrenia.

All of this sets the stage for severe misperceptions about schizophrenia within biblical counseling, which was not corrected, or so presumed to have been corrected, until very recently in ACBC's history. However, no one has said that Jay Adams was wrong, and no one expresses regret over his opinions on the matter, to my knowledge. So, I am very reserved in my opinion that there has been the change necessary. At the same time, Charles Hodges's lecture at the 2014 ACBC conference actually sounded very appropriate. He referred to schizophrenia as a medical problem with pathology, not a sin problem like Jay Adams had done in 1976.

Other authors in the biblical counseling movement have, since its beginnings, referred to schizophrenia in the same way as Adams. A doctor of ministry dissertation entitled "A Christian Counselor's Experience in Working with Schizophrenics in the State Hospital System and Preliminary Treatment Suggestions" by James R. Eichelberger, written in 1987 for the faculty at Westminster Theological Seminary, blatantly calls biblical counselors to confront the sinful delusions that the patients entertain. However, Charles Hodges in the previously mentioned 2014 ACBC conference apparently did none of this and, I hope, does not believe this to be appropriate.

So it is likely that a certain degree of certified biblical counselors still affirm Jay Adams's original insights into this disease. Again, as a

---

[27] Jay Adams, "The Christian Approach to Schizophrenia," *Journal of Biblical Counseling* 14, no. 1 (fall 1995): 28.

case in point, I myself was told while in the army while awaiting medical discharge that if I dealt with my relationship problems, I would deal with my schizophrenia. Misperceptions still exist. However, where biblical counseling can still be an asset is in spiritual and moral guidance to someone with schizophrenia. There have been times when prayer was greatly helpful to me as I struggled with delusions, such as "there are cameras in my room." The presence of God gave me someone to talk out my delusions to even then.

The point is that prayer helps, personal guidance helps, and the Bible helps. Even psychologists and psychiatrists know the benefits of spiritual guidance in dealing with these issues. At the same time, actual therapy for a schizophrenic individual is very helpful from a psychologist or, by extension, an integrationist who has studied not only the psychology of a schizophrenic but their treatment. This whole issue of whether to rely on soul care or therapy is rooted in whether or not schizophrenia is a medical issue or a spiritual issue. The soul is in control of the body, but the soul, at the same time, is greatly limited or inhibited by the physical body in ways that no one fully understands.

The body and the soul were made to be one, and they interact and are dependent on each other. As a result, schizophrenia is principally rooted in biological processes that doctors and scientists do not yet fully understand, as Hodges pointed out in his lecture at the 2014 conference. After all, neither soul care nor therapy has been really presented as a real cure for this illness. It is probably safe to assume that if counseling from either side is not the solution, then the problem is not principally the soul of man. Soul care and therapy have been known to help though. The former from biblical counselors or pastors and the latter from licensed psychologists.

PART 4
What We as Laymen and Ministers Can Do for Them

CHAPTER 6

Meditation and the Nature of Mental Illness

I have been encouraged to research puritanical meditation for practical help in developing a guide for how to treat mental illness from a biblical perspective. I believe that there are good materials out there that reference the puritans and speak to practical steps to meditation that is thoroughly biblical and nonmystical. Well, I could reference one in particular that I read from. I believe that there is work that the biblical counseling movement could do in this regard that would be beneficial. I don't want to do that in this book.

I believe that the most helpful thing in dealing with a schizophrenic or any mentally ill person is to be very grounded in the ABCs of Christian life and character and to encourage the mentally ill, whatever their diagnosis is, to persevere. A minister should acknowledge the difficulty of the individual's dilemma and encourage him or her to love Jesus and listen to Him. It is very simple.

We could delve deeply into puritanical devotions that could yield some increase, but the bottom line is that we memorize scripture, even just phrases if a person can only manage small amounts, think about theological realities, and consider good examples of these lived out in the lives of others.

Adam W. Lambdin

1. Memorize Scripture

If you can encourage a mentally ill person to memorize scripture, you can use that scripture as a hook to hang encouragement on that can do amazing things for them. I would start by creating a brief lesson where you read the passage in context and walk the individual through it, talking about it using not just the grammatical-historical method that we learn in school, but use your life as an example and what it means to you (not in the "it's all relative sense" but in a practical, daily sense). You can draw on other people's lives in your church or in church history. It doesn't matter, but make it real. Make it simple. Pray through the passage with the mentally ill person. Do it not just to teach but to inspire with hope. Pick uplifting passages and stories.

John MacArthur used to speak of "sermonettes for Christianettes" as a bad thing, and I agree, but in this case, you are using something very basic and simple and possibly short for great purposes. Have the person memorize even just a phrase or one verse or two verses, depending on the person, and tell them to recite it to themselves whenever they feel tempted to, for example, believe something that is not true. One verse that you may find helpful too in dealing with auditory hallucinations is 1 Corinthians 2:11, which says, "For who among men knows the thoughts of a man except the spirit of the man which is in him?" In other words, people can't read your mind or send and receive "mental messages." There is no ESP, and at the same time, you can draw out lessons from the actual context.

2. Think about Theological Realities

Be sure to encourage them with doctrine. You can hang these truths on the convenient mental hooks of memorized scripture that you have previously given them to regurgitate in their daily lives. Feel free to be a little preachy. Some people really like it. They need to hear the truth about life and character and Christ-likeness. And be patient! All of these steps could be repeating lessons that go on for their whole lives with very gradual growth. You just don't know what to expect. I'm not saying that there can't be growth, just that it could possibly be very gradual.

3. Consider Good Examples

The last thing to do in any full dish of pastoral encouragement is in referencing the good examples of people who live this stuff out. People need good examples, and they need to see the struggle and the shortfalls and the victories all together. People love good stories of good practical heroes. They use stuff like this in psych wards too. I've seen it firsthand, whether it was a movie or a little group therapy talk about a historical person. It's inspiration. Pass it on.

What Really Helps

In regards to medication, I have met an individual, for example, who I think could really benefit from psychotropic meds. I am not sure that he is encouraged by his church to look into taking it or not. The way he talks would make me think not, but I know that he would benefit from them based on the obscure and somewhat cryptic ways that he sometimes talks and by his lack of ability to get ahead in life. I do get the impression from our brief past encounters that he is opposed to taking them.

I know of another family who has two sons that are schizophrenic but who won't permit their sons to take psychotropic medication because they believe that it is a spiritual battle, not a physical one. And on the list goes of people refusing very real and practical help that could for all practical purposes save the lives of their loved ones or themselves because of the nature of mental illness as being physical.

Medication is oftentimes the very necessary first step in dealing with people like myself. The people who recover on their own simply never had the illness or are superficially pronounced "normal" due to prejudiced views against the need for taking meds in the first place.

There needs to be a realistic grasp of the need for medication. Perhaps it doesn't even need to be something that they are dependent on their whole lives, but it could be useful in the short run as well. There are too many anti-psychiatrists out there who follow in the line of Thomas Szasz and others, at least in the confines of my own counseling studies. And here I am, someone totally dependent on my daily dose of meds and with an otherwise totally normal life to say so.

Notes from *Saving Normal*

The best secular book that I have read on the nature of mental illness is the book called *Saving Normal* by Allen Frances. If I had my way, every biblical counseling school in the country would require its students to read it. It offers a very balanced perspective on the problems of psychiatry in America and its benefits. Dr. Frances outlines three different approaches to the nature of mental illness using the idea of "Three Umpires."

Umpire 1:

> "There are balls and there are strikes and I call them as they are" ... [He] Believes that mental disorders are real "diseases" ... Umpire One has great faith in our ability to detect the true essence of things ... Dozens of different candidate genes have been "found," but in follow-up studies each turned out to be fool's gold. Mental disorders are too heterogeneous in presentation and in causality to be considered simple diseases; instead each of our currently defined disorders will eventually turn out to be many different diseases. For now at least, Umpire One has been called out on strikes.[28]

---

[28] Allen Frances, *Saving Normal* (New York, New York: HarperCollins Publishers, 2013), 19.

Umpire 2:

"There are balls and there are strikes and I call them as I see them." Umpire Two [believes] that they [mental illnesses] are something in between—useful constructs that provide no more (but no less) than a best current guess on how to sort psychiatric distress … Umpire Two has the firmest grasp on elusive reality, paradoxically because he understands and accepts that we can know it only partially. Of course, reality is "protean"—constantly changing shape and hard to hold. No doubt there is an enormous gap between things as they really are and things as we perceive them—not just in psychiatry. Only 4 percent of our known universe can be directly detected by our senses—the rest of its energy and matter remaining "dark" to us. The quantum world is so weirdly discordant with our own that even the physicists who can mathematically predict its every characteristic cannot find an intuitive way to relate to it. And how can light manage to be a wave that suddenly turns into a particle just when we choose to look at it a certain way.

… Our classification of mental disorders is no more than a collection of fallible and limited constructs that seeks but never finds the truth—but this remains our best current way of communicating about, treating, and researching mental disorders.[29]

---

[29] Allen Frances, *Saving Normal* (New York, New York: HarperCollins Publishers, 2013), 19–21.

Umpire 3:

"There are no balls and no strikes until I call them" … Umpire three [believes] that they are fanciful "myths" … Umpire three presents … the skeptical and solipsistic doubt that man can ever catch protean reality by the tail and know things as they truly are. He would argue that mental disorders are no more than arbitrary and sometimes noxious "myths" … Though not a discrete "disease entity" (like, say, a brain tumor or a stroke), schizophrenia produces profound and prolonged "dis-ease"—that is, distress and incapacity. The patterns of its presentation are clearly recognizable, can be reliably diagnosed, run in families, have brain imaging correlates, predict course, and respond to specific treatments. Schizophrenia is real enough and no psychiatric invention for those who suffer from it and for their loved ones.[30]

So there you have Allen Frances's take on the issue, and I feel that he is essentially right. I feel that there are a lot of biblical counselors that I have met, certainly not all of them and possibly not most of them, that are in on Umpire Three's perspective. That is where biblical counseling started under Jay Adams, but that is not necessarily where it is now. I do not feel that I am in the position to say where exactly biblical counseling is now, and I don't want to be at odds with anyone. I have no desire to get in an argument with persons who take any kind of a stance in any regard to the above. I am merely presenting it as what I personally see as an objective perspective.

---

[30] Allen Frances, *Saving Normal* (New York, New York: HarperCollins Publishers, 2013), 19–20.

CHAPTER 7

The Encouragement That a Schizophrenic Needs from the Bible

While I was schizophrenic and before I was in the army and diagnosed, before many of the troubles that I experienced, I was asked to preach a sermon at my parents' home church. It was very early in my schizophrenia and before all of my battles with people began to come out. I knew instinctively that spiritual stability was the most important subject area for me to grow in personally even though I had no knowledge of my condition at the time. So I worked hard to prepare a sermon on Philippians 4:1–9 because I wanted that passage more than anything else to be ingrained in my mind. I was preaching first to myself.

It was my first sermon ever, and when I would preach a second time several years later after my diagnosis and prescription and being in several psych wards, I just had to preach it again to myself from another pulpit on a Sunday night at my new home church. I borrowed a great deal from my mentor, John MacArthur. A lot of the framework and direction of the sermon comes from his series of sermons on the same passage.

Don't assume that you can only minister to a schizophrenic while they are medicated. Encouragement and positive, accurate instruction from the Bible is appropriate all of the time, no matter what. It can possibly correct their behavior and guide their thinking because the Word of God is sufficient to do all this, even when a person is delusional. Of course, without medication, they will still be delusional, but you can greatly aid them and correct possible behaviors with the simple encouragement from the Word. Don't focus on trying to make him or her not delusional; just focus on encouraging them to act in a way that pleases God. However, I am not saying that you should avoid encouraging them to see a psychiatrist. This should be done immediately if you suspect that such a person is having problems due to a possible psychiatric condition. But there is no substitute for the Word of God.

The following is my transcript in full, and I believe that it is directly applicable to your support of and counseling of schizophrenic persons. I personally would encourage them to memorize it as well as other passages. I would encourage them to make it their theme verse against all the false thinking that they will be forced to confront, and I would focus on simply being friends with them at the same time. It will involve a lot of patience. I hope that the following sermon will serve to encourage those who suffer with mental illness who might read my book.

The Sermon

Philippians 4:1–9 says the following:

> Therefore, my beloved brethren whom I long to see, my joy and crown, in this way stand firm in the Lord, my beloved. I urge Euodia and I urge Syntyche to live in harmony in the Lord. Indeed, true companion, I ask you also to help these women who have shared my struggle in the cause of the gospel, together with Clement also and the rest of my fellow workers, whose names are in the book of life. Rejoice in the Lord always; again I will say, rejoice! Let your gentle spirit be known to all men. The Lord is near. Be anxious for nothing, but in everything by prayer and

supplication with thanksgiving let your requests be made known to God. And the peace of God, which surpasses all comprehension, will guard your hearts and your minds in Christ Jesus. Finally, brethren, whatever is true, whatever is honorable, whatever is right, whatever is pure, whatever is lovely, whatever is of good repute, if there is any excellence and if anything worthy of praise, dwell on these things. The things you have learned and received and heard and seen in me, practice these things, and the God of peace will be with you.

I really believe that all of us want to be stable people. We talk with high esteem for those men and women who are firm and strong in their convictions and in their character. No one wants to be known as unstable, as someone who is basically a weakling or a whiner. Stories that we love lift up the strong and the victorious. We want to exemplify that same firm and unshakable character.

What has become one of my favorite poems, called "If" by Rudyard Kipling, goes like this:

> If you can keep your head when all about you
> Are losing theirs and blaming it on you;
> If you can trust yourself when all men doubt you,
> But make allowance for their doubting too;
> If you can wait and not be tired by waiting,
> Or, being lied about, don't deal in lies,
> Or, being hated, don't give way to hating,
> And yet don't look too good, nor talk too wise;
>
> If you can dream—and not make dreams your master;
> If you can think—and not make thoughts your aim;
> If you can meet with triumph and disaster
> And treat those two imposters just the same;

Adam W. Lambdin

> If you can bear to hear the truth you've spoken
> Twisted by knaves to make a trap for fools,
> Or watch the things you gave your life to broken,
> And stoop and build 'em up with wornout tools;
>
> If you can talk with crowds and keep your virtue,
> Or walk with kings—nor lose the common touch;
> If neither foes nor loving friends can hurt you;
> If all men count with you, but none too much;
> If you can fill the unforgiving minute
> With sixty seconds' worth of distance run -
> Yours is the Earth and everything that's in it,
> And—which is more—you'll be a Man my son![31]

    Rudyard Kipling knew that real manhood was about being sure and stable even when the worst comes knocking at your door. And, as a side note, we know spiritually that we are making real progress in our spiritual lives when our back is against the wall and we respond instinctively with strength and assurance. We know that because it's one thing to respond well when we can prepare ourselves and think about how we're going to respond, but it is another thing when our instincts, which arise from our hearts, are set loose on the impulse arising from the moment, when our world may collapse, so to speak, or when something bad happens, and on the turn of a dime we respond with strength. That's when we know that we are making progress in this. So, what is the key to having this kind of spiritual strength?

    The issue that Paul here addresses in the life of the Philippian believers is that of spiritual stability. He says in verse one, "Stand fast in the Lord, beloved." That is his command. What follows is how we are supposed to fulfill this command.

    The context from which Paul speaks here is out of the doctrine

---

[31] Poetry Foundation, "If," Retrieved October 4, 2016 from www.poetryfoundation.org/poems-and-poets/poems/detal/46473.

of the church. The signature word for the book of Philippians is joy. Paul uses this word to describe these believers and their fellowship to him. This passage and the issues that it addresses are not written to a church that is in some form of disobedience or sin per se. The Philippians were actually supporting Paul and sharing in his ministry so that he over and over again expresses thanks, but even though the Philippians were demonstrating these qualities, they struggled with common sins that any church faces. They were struggling with bickering, anxiety, and there was a lack of peace and stability in some minds. So, Paul transitions over from teaching about the church to addressing the ordinary needs of these believers. He says in verse 1: "Therefore, my beloved brethren whom I long to see, my joy and crown, in this way stand firm in the Lord, beloved."

The word used for "stand" in verse 1 is the same used in Ephesians 6:13 that we "stand" against the wiles of the devil. He also uses this word in 1 Corinthians 16:13 where he says, "Be on the alert, stand firm in the faith …" Likewise, Paul here says that the Philippians are to stand in the doctrines that he has just explained—that is, that we ought to be pressing toward the goal of the upward call of God just as he is (v. 14), and that our citizenship is not on earth but in heaven, which Jesus Christ will accomplish when He transforms our lowly bodies to be conformed to His glorious body.

Believers are to stand in the truth as a soldier prepared to be firm in the gospel as in Ephesians 6. He speaks right into the heart of the situation in Philippi that the Christians here stand in the Spirit-filled confidence that right thinking produces. You as Christians are to have these qualities as characteristic of your life. Even as you have demonstrated obedience in your walk, Paul is calling us to bring our lives even more closely in line with Christ. Under this exhortation, he gives six imperatives for how to live a spiritually stable life. They are:

1. Be Unified
2. Be Rejoicing
3. Be Gentle

4. Be Praying
5. Be Focused
6. Be Practicing

1. Be Unified (vv. 2-3)

> "I urge Euodia and I urge Syntyche to live in harmony in the Lord. Indeed, true companion, I ask you also to help these women who have shared my struggle in the cause of the gospel, together with Clement also and the rest of my fellow workers, whose names are in the book of life."

Paul turns to these two women, Euodia and Syntyche, and tells them to live in love and harmony. These were two women who possibly hosted gatherings or were in some way prominent in the church. Their argument could have been over the simplest thing, and no one else was taking the initiative to deal with it, but it was causing friction in the body. They were suffering from pride, and this caused them to leave self-sacrifice behind.

Paul turns to "true companion." He uses the Greek word for "true" and says "true yokefellow." Some argue that this is an unidentified person that Paul is simply identifying as a true companion familiar to all, but others argue that this is a proper name and that Paul is here emphasizing the fact that suzugos is being a true suzugos, or a true yokefellow. He is living up to his name. I actually believe it is a proper name just like Barnabas was a proper name and meant "son of encouragement." It is just like Paul said that Onesimos, which means "useful," has become "useful" to both Philemon and to himself.

Further on, he asks that Clement together with the rest of the saints help these women who have labored with him. Paul asks these men to "help these women who have shared" in his work and fellowship of the gospel to put themselves under that same commitment in this case. Lloyd-Jones points out that this admonition was given within the context of his instruction about the church. Paul doesn't simply command them per se, but he admonishes them out of the context of doctrine. In other words, "Here's what the church is; here's what the church should be; and therefore be unified." It is not a harsh remark but an exhortation that the church deal with this issue in a way so as to bring harmony. Its basis is found, for example, earlier in Philippians where Paul says that our citizenship is not on earth but in heaven.

When personalities abrade one another in the church, it is often, if not always, the direct result of barriers built up because of conflicting interests. One person says, "I want to do things this way," and another person says, "I want to do it this way," and the end of these things is conflict, bitterness, or what have you—spiritual instability.

But the heart of a Christian should put others' interests above his own in order to preserve unity. For instance, Romans 14 says:

> Now accept the one who is weak in faith, but not for the purpose of passing judgment on his opinions. One person has faith that he may eat all things, but he who is weak eats vegetables only. The one who eats is not to regard with contempt the one who does not eat, and the one who does not eat is not to judge the one who eats, for God has accepted him. Who are you to judge the servant of another? To his own master he stands or falls; and he will stand, for the Lord is able to make him stand. One person regards one day above another, another regards every day alike Each person must be fully convinced in his own mind. He who observes the day, observes it for the Lord, and he who eats, does so for the Lord, for he gives thanks to God; and he who eats not, for the Lord he does not eat, and gives thanks to God. For not one of us lives for himself, and not one dies for himself; for if we live, we live for the Lord, or if we

die, we die for the Lord; therefore whether we live or die, we are the Lord's.

You can argue over the smallest nonsensical things until you drown everyone else in your drama, but here Paul says that the Philippians, and particularly Euodia and Syntyche, must set aside personal preference for the sake of the other. Why? Romans 14:9 says, "For to this end Christ died and lived again, that He might be Lord ..." and verse 10, "... we will all stand before the judgment seat of God." God is the judge of both parties. Real submission to God says He is judge, and we don't need to argue about little things.

And as a side note, isn't it true that we feel a lot better and more secure when we know that we are getting along with everyone at church? If you know in a spiritual sense, *Everyone at church has my back, and I have theirs*, then that is a guaranteed element of real spiritual stability. The key to this is self-sacrifice for the sake of others as opposed to arguing, as Euodia and Syntyche are doing here. If you want to be a spiritually stable person, you ought to put getting along with fellow believers on the top of your priority list. This leads from the first point, be unified, and to the second point, be rejoicing.

2. Be Rejoicing (v. 4)

"Rejoice in the Lord always; again I will way, rejoice!"

What does Paul mean by "rejoice!"? He is not talking necessarily about a giddy, happy kind of person who is perpetually grinning and glad. For example, 1 Thessalonians 5:18 says, "In everything give thanks, for this is God's will for you in Christ Jesus." Paul is referring to an inner gratitude and constant thankfulness to the Lord that rises above all else. And when we as Christians stop and think about it, there are many reasons why our attitude should be no less. There are three reasons why we ought to rejoice:

a. We should rejoice because of our salvation.

In Psalm 103:1–12 David writes:

> Bless the Lord, O my soul,
> And all that is within me, bless His holy name.
> Bless the Lord, O my soul,
> And forget none of His benefits;
> Who pardons all your iniquities,
> Who heals all your diseases;
> Who redeems your life from the pit,
> Who crowns you with lovingkindness and compassion;
> Who satisfies your years with good things,
> So that your youth is renewed like the eagle.
> The Lord performs righteous deeds
> And judgments for all who are oppressed.
> He made known His ways to Moses,
> His acts to the sons of Israel.
> The Lord is compassionate and gracious,
> Slow to anger and abounding in lovingkindness.
> He will not always strive with us,
> Nor will He keep His anger forever.
> He has not dealt with us according to our sins,
> Nor rewarded us according to our iniquities.
> For as high as the heavens are above the earth,
> So great is His lovingkindness toward those who fear Him.
> As far as the east is from the west,
> So far has He removed our transgressions from us.

God has promised that, in Christ, He has pardoned our iniquities and healed our diseases, and crowned us with loving kindness and compassion, and "as far as the east is from the west so far has He removed our transgressions from us." We know that no matter what pain, or heartache, or suffering, God has completely removed the penalty of our sin far from us. We stand forgiven. Even if the worst should happen, we are assured a place in heaven. I have heard it said that the worst that could happen is that we would die. I disagree. I think death is, as John Piper says, like my car; it takes me where I want to go. The worst that could happen is that we would live on in the flesh, right? But God is a God of deliverance, and He will rescue us from living on in the flesh forever, right? Eventually that place in heaven will be fully realized.

Another reason we should rejoice is:

b. We should rejoice because God is sovereign.

Romans 8:28 teaches us that "God causes all things [both good and bad] to work together for good to those who love God, to those who are called according to His purpose." Inherent in this verse is the conviction that God is good, right? How could we expect that a sovereign God would work all things together for good unless He himself is good and sovereign? A good God who is immanently sovereign over all things is working in each individual life for the purpose of good. I can't think of a more encouraging truth for me or anyone. God has you right where He wants you to be today. That is the most encouraging truth imaginable. The simple fact that God has sovereignly placed you exactly where He wants you to be today in this moment is an unstoppable truth in preparing us for spiritual stability. His plan of sanctification is literally being unfolded in your life by each person in your life and by each circumstance in your life. He has made no mistakes in your life leading to this moment. You might have made mistakes, but God has made none at all. His sovereign plan for your good is literally unfolding right now. Isn't that encouraging?

Philippians 1:6 says, "For I am confident of this very thing, that He who began a good work in you will perfect it until the day of Christ Jesus." We know that God has the ultimate goal of glorification in mind and that our lives are progressing toward that end now.

One concept that is sometimes very difficult for us to grasp is how we can rejoice when under persecution, just as Matthew 5 says, "blessed are those who have been persecuted for the sake of righteousness, for theirs is the kingdom of heaven." Paul says in Philippians 1 verses 12–18 that His circumstances had turned out for the furtherance of the gospel. Even his enemies had began to compete with him, as it were, thinking to advance their names above his own. But his response is in verse 17, "the former proclaim Christ out of selfish ambition rather than from pure motives, thinking to cause me distress in my imprisonment. What then? Only that in every way, whether in pretense or in truth, Christ is proclaimed; and in this I rejoice." Paul's secret to spiritual stability is concentrated in those verses. He had so disconnected his joy from himself and his circumstances and had fixed them instead to the Lord that it didn't matter what happened to him so long as Christ received the glory. Wow. What an attitude. If you want to be spiritually stable, don't care so much about yourself. Care about how Christ is glorified. That leads to our third reason we should rejoice, and that is we should rejoice because of the hope of heaven.

c. We should rejoice because of the hope of heaven.

A pastor in the Soviet Union by the name of Richard Wurmbrand suffered fourteen years in prison. Wurmbrand was at different times put in a refrigerator, taken out to thaw, and put back inside again. He was starved, beaten, had holes drilled in his legs, and in all this, he remained faithful to God and even spoke of moments of joy in prison.

Wurmbrand endured fourteen years of torment for Christ and came out with an expression of joy that held him through the darkness. How can one maintain this kind of joy under these circumstances? Two things from Wurmbrand: the joy of preaching the gospel and secondly, the hope of heaven. In thinking about the glories of heaven, he recounted an argument that the church used in refuting atheism, which is about a human embryo, and applied it to his circumstances:

> ... if the embryo could think, he would say to himself, "here arms grow on me. I do not need them. I cannot even stretch them. Why do they grow? Perhaps they grow for a future stage of my existence, in which I will have to work with them. Legs grow, but I have to keep them bent toward my chest. Why do they grow? Probably life in a large world follows, where I will have to walk. Eyes grow, although I am surrounded by perfect darkness and don't need them. Why do I have eyes? Probably a world with light and colors will follow."
>
> So, if the embryo would reflect on his own development, he would know about a life outside of his mother's womb, without having seen it. It is the same with us. As long as we are young, we have vigor, but no mind to use it properly. When, with the years, we have grown in knowledge and wisdom, the hearse waits to take us to the grave. Why was it necessary to grow in a knowledge and wisdom that we can use no more? Why do arms, legs, and eyes grow on an embryo? It is for what follows. So it is with us here. We grow here in experience, knowledge, and wisdom for what follows. We are prepared to serve on a higher level that follows death.[32]

If he went through what he did and came out from it joyful, then there is validity in his reasoning. If a heavenward perspective stood through those things, then it will stand through less in our lives. Do you ever stop and consider that the difficulties and troubles of this life are working in you things that you, yourself, will not be able to fully utilize or appreciate until you are really free to use these gifts in

---

[32] Richard Wurmbrand, *Tortured for Christ* (Living Sacrifice Book Company, 1998), 88.

heaven? Sometimes, there is no apparent reason why we suffer but to cause us to more fully appreciate the glory of heaven and to use our gifts there for the everlasting glory of God.

However, as inspiring as Wurmbrand's story is, the challenge in our context is vastly different. We live with lives that are very comfortable and free from that kind of suffering. Our lives consist of work, home, family, and the daily routines of life. These things can possibly drag us down. For us, the issue is very much an issue of simple endurance. How do you maintain a spirit of joy when the reality of your humble life is that you just want to maintain the spirit of stability in the midst of the ups and downs of regular life?

Our struggles can be very humbling when our attitudes are so out of key. Our challenge is stewardship. We have been given stewardship of the things that God has given to us while trying to maintain a heart of gratitude and a joy fixed heavenward. Paul encourages us here with this command to rejoice in the Lord. It may be in a different context, but it is the same principle at work in each individual. We can rejoice in the hope of heaven.

The third principle for spiritual stability is to be gentle.

3. Be Gentle (v. 5)

> "Let your gentle spirit be known to all men. The Lord is near."

Here, Paul's focus is not only on gentleness but on forbearance, deference, or graciousness. It is a distinguishing mark of our character as Christians. We are to give preference to another's good above our own. This strikes at the heart of who we should be as Christians. We might immediately ask, what is the source of this strength? As the context shows, we are to do this "in the Lord." What is the greatest example of sweet forbearance in the Bible? Jesus Christ. He was the master of gracious forbearance.

In 1 Peter 2:23, it says, "And while being reviled, He did not revile in return; while suffering, He uttered no threats, but kept entrusting Himself to Him who judges righteously."

Christ continually entrusted Himself to Him who judges righteously. It is not a matter of gritting your teeth and bearing with it but of a sweet committing of oneself to the Lord. It is a continual submitting of oneself to God's purpose because He is sovereign. Nothing matters but that God is in control, and I can, as a result, trust and rest in that knowledge no matter what.

There is a difference between the stoic forbearance and the Christian forbearance. It is not a matter, again, of tolerating life but of living life for the glory of God. There is eternal value in being the kind of person that Christ was, who perfectly exemplified godly character to the end. Probably one of the hardest things for us as humans to learn is how to accept less than what we are due. Especially in our own times when we are supposed to maintain a healthy self-esteem. Self-esteem says that we should have it, whether it be that promotion or that reputation or what have you, because we deserve that. However, when we are looking at ourselves in light of the value of Christ, then we know that we as individuals are far from worthy and should, because of that, strive to imitate His perfect example.

It doesn't mean anything other than that we must make ourselves committed to serve and to sacrifice for the good of others. Paul admonishes the Philippians to live this out. If you want to be spiritually stable, have a graciousness and forbearance that transcends this world just as Jesus Christ did. Paul then adds the fourth principle of spiritual stability, be praying.

4. Be Praying (v. 6)

> "Be anxious for nothing, but in everything by prayer and supplication with thanksgiving let your requests be made known to God. And the peace of God, which surpasses all comprehension, will guard your hearts and your minds in Christ Jesus."

The call here to be anxious for nothing is given with a clear road to deal with the how of that command. We could just say straight out, "Be anxious for nothing," because the truth is that we simply can't change anything by worrying about it anyway, right? But that is simplistic and does not get to the root of the matter. He says be anxious for nothing, and then Paul says, "Here's how."

Paul adds that all things should be submitted to God with prayer and supplication. If you surrender your situation to the sovereignty of God, then you are placing the situation outside of your control and putting it in God's control. You might say that the problem is one that directly involves you and your action, but here's something Marty Holdaman has pointed out in our small group Bible study before. He has said, "Don't you think that if God wanted to stop whatever it was that happened in your life, He could have stopped it?" The fact is God allows things for a reason. He never is thrown off guard by our misdeeds or errors. And you always have the opportunity to come back from error and redirect your life to right thinking and living. You may even do it even stronger than you otherwise would have. What happens when you get a broken arm? The wound heals back stronger than what it was before. Don't be discouraged too much even by your own sin and failures; just come back with greater assurance of God's providence at work in your life. You can know that He is doing good in you.

Paul makes both the command and the means exhaustive. He says both that we should be anxious for nothing and that we should submit everything by prayer and supplication. This means that there is nothing that God can allow to take place in your life that cannot be rightly approached simply by doing so with prayer and supplication, nothing.

Again, the image is of spiritual stability, spiritual security, and peace. Verse 7 says, "And the peace of God, which surpasses all comprehension, will guard your hearts and your minds in Christ Jesus." What is the result of this obedience? The promise that Paul gives is that the peace of God will guard your heart if you submit the situation up to Him.

The book of Habakkuk illustrates this. Habakkuk is in Judah in the midst of her rebellion. And he asks God a series of questions beginning in chapter 1. He asks the Lord, in chapter 1, why he himself is allowed to see violence, destruction, and evil and the Lord does not intervene.

God continues through the later part of chapter 2 showing that the Chaldeans will be a punishment unto themselves and will destroy themselves as a people, but God's answer to the prophet is in verse 4, "the righteous will live by his faith." Habakkuk responds to this in faith. He has just the perfect attitude at the end in 3:17–19:

> Though the fig tree should not blossom
> And there be no fruit on the vines,
> Though the yield of the olive should fail
> And the fields produce no food,
> Though the flock should be cut off from the fold
> And there be no cattle in the stalls,
> Yet I will exult in the Lord,
> I will rejoice in the God of my salvation.
> The Lord God is my strength,
> And He has made my feet like hinds' feet,
> And makes me walk on my high places.

Habakkuk lastly rests on the fact that his faith and his trust is in the Lord whatever the circumstance may be. He doesn't need to fear what God has ordained. Why? Because God is good, right? Spiritual stability is found when we have a firm confidence that God works it all together for our good and His glory. End of story. God sees the end from the beginning, and He knows we're going to be fine. Don't collapse under the pressure of life. Don't respond with increased anxiety. Be firm in the principle, like Habakkuk, that, though the worst should happen, I will have confidence in the God of my salvation. Do you have that kind of confidence? Or are you overly anxious and worried about the state of the American economy and where it's going, for example? Habakkuk had it right.

5. Be Focused (v. 8)

"Finally, brethren, whatever is true, whatever is honorable, whatever is right, whatever is pure, whatever is lovely, whatever is of good repute, if there is any excellence and if anything worthy of praise, dwell on these things."

The Greek word means simply "let your mind dwell on." The principle is that the believers be absorbed in thoughts that are true, honorable, right, pure, lovely, of good repute, of excellence, or in anything worthy of praise. This is not just a nice list of abstract things that Paul wants the Philippians to ponder for fun. He is exhorting them to have minds disciplined to dwell on things that are purposed toward living them out effectively.

I do not believe that you, as a believer, are being obedient to this passage if you say that you think about these things but do not live them out. Are you really supposed to just think about good things in a general sense, and yet your life tells us something else? You do live consistently with your thoughts. If you think on what is good, if you're focused on it, you will do good. Conversely, if you think on that which is evil, Mark 7:21–23 says, "For from within, out of the heart of men, proceed the evil thoughts, fornications, thefts, murders, adulteries, deeds of coveting and wickedness, as well as deceit, sensuality, envy, slander, pride and foolishness. All these evil things proceed from within and defile the man."

There is no life in the ungodly because there is no life within their minds. They are excluded because of the absence of God's life. On the other hand, we are commanded in 1 Peter 1:13 to "prepare your minds for action." We as believers are to exercise disciplined minds to the purpose of bringing God glory. So, think about "whatever is true, whatever is honorable, whatever is right, whatever is pure, whatever is lovely, whatever is of good repute; if there is any excellence and if is anything worthy of praise, dwell on these things. This will yield great spiritual stability and victory in your life. This leads to the next point in Paul's message, be practicing.

6. Be Practicing (v. 9)

> "The things you have learned and received and heard and seen in me, practice these things, and the God of peace will be with you."

Paul writes that the Philippians follow in his footsteps in what they have learned, received, heard, and seen. You've heard the saying, "like people, like priest." When you get down to it, the people are often no better than the pastor leading them. And just as we all as Christians need godly role models in our lives, Paul says here that the Philippians are to practice the things that they have observed in his life.

The Greek word for "learned" comes from the word for disciple. The Philippian believers were the disciples of Paul, who likewise told Timothy in 2 Timothy 1:13 to follow him as he followed Christ: "Retain the standard of sound words which you have heard from me, in the faith and love which are in Christ Jesus." Paul had thus established himself in following the person and character of Christ.

Christianity is more than simple head knowledge. There are many people who are primarily concerned with the abstract and with theology, who maybe even know the Bible frontwards and backwards, but they lack in crucial areas of their lives that should be in conformity to Christ.

At the heart of any Christian's pursuit is the knowledge of God. He is our creator; He knows our frame. He is our sustainer, and He will accomplish the purpose that He's begun. His purpose is that we would fulfill ours in being conformed to the image of His son. Paul has reiterated this again and again to the Philippians, and this principle undergirds the commands listed here.

This is what produces spiritual stability. In essence, it is commitment to a God that is good and sovereign and who wants us to be unified as believers, be rejoicing in the Lord, be gentle, be praying and submitting all things to God, be focused on what is God-honoring, and be practicing what others have done before us.

These are the keys to spiritual stability in our lives. But let me just say that the key motivation and the key principle that I find encouraging is that God calls us to rejoice in Him. God is good and sovereign, and He has placed me today exactly where He wants me. There are no mistakes. If I know this, then things don't take me by surprise really. "Oh, an interruption in my day? That was predetermined. An illness in my life? God has an overshadowing purpose." And you know what? God is a God of deliverance, and if He won't deliver us in this life, then He will by bringing us to the next. And this life is only preparing me to appreciate eternity in a very real and incredible way that I can't imagine or fully appreciate now.

So persevere. Pray when you're discouraged to a God who has a perfect plan for you. Think about doctrine and the things that are edifying, and your mind will be fully prepared to encounter whatever life has for you. Practice the things essential for godliness and be unified as believers. Have fellowship with God and man.

Charles Spurgeon said, "Remember this, had any other condition been better for you than the one in which you are, divine love would have put you there. You are placed by God in the most suitable circumstances, and if you had the choosing of your lot, you would soon cry, 'Lord, choose my inheritance for me, for by my self-will I am pierced through with many sorrows.'"[33]

There is nothing better for us than what we have, in an eternal sense. Spiritual stability is based on being unified in the church, rejoicing in God and all that He has done for us, being gentle and forbearing in our response to people and to life, being prayerful when things get hard, being focused on virtue in our hearts, and lastly on practicing the examples set before us. This is how we can be more than stable. We can be spiritually strong.

---

[33] Heartlight.Org, "Evening Devotion, Nov. 11th," retrieved October 4, 2016 from www.heartlight.org/spurgeon/1111-pm.html.

Bibliography

Chapter 1

Frances, Allen. *Saving Normal.* New York, NY: HarperCollins Publishers, 2013.

Chapter 4

Berman, Karen, and David Daniel, and Daniel Weinberger. *Comprehensive Textbook of Psychiatry VI.* Edited by Harold I. Kaplan and Benjamin J. Sadock. Baltimore, MD: Williams and Wilkins, 1995.

Cannon, Tyrone D. *Origins and Development of Schizophrenia.* Edited by Mark F. Lenzwenweger and Robert H. Dworkin. Washington, DC: American Psychological Association, 1998.

Carpenter, William T. and Robert W. Buchanan. *Comprehensive Textbook of Psychiatry VI.* Edited by Harold I. Kaplan and Benjamin J. Sadock. Baltimore, MD: Williams and Wilkins, 1995.

Dorland's Medical Dictionary for Health Consumers. S.v. "paresis." Retrieved April 3, 2015 from http://medical-dictionary.thefreedictionary.com/paresis.

Hermann, Richard. "Schizophrenia: Clinical Manifestations, Course, Assessment, and Diagnosis" UpToDate.Com, July 26, 2013. Accessed February 24, 2015 at http://www.uptodate.

com/contents/schizophrenia-clinical-manifestations-course-assessment-and-diagnosis.
Gottesman, Irving I. and Steven O. Moldin. *Origins and Development of Schizophrenia*. Edited by Mark F. Lenzwenweger and Robert H. Dworkin. Washington, DC: American Psychological Association, 1998.
Hodges, Charles. "Schizophrenia." 2014 ACBC Annual Conference—Mental Illness.
MedicineNet.Com. "Definition of Gliosis." Last modified June 14, 2012. Accessed April 2, 2015 at http://www.medicinenet.com/script/main/art.asp?articlekey=25457.
Szasz, Thomas. "Mental Illness Is Still a Myth." *Journal of Biblical Counseling* 14, no. 1 (fall 1995).
Welch, Edward T. *Blame It on the Brain*. Phillisburg, New Jersey: P and R Publishing, 1998.

Chapter 5

Adams, Jay. "The Christian Approach to Schizophrenia." *Journal of Biblical Counseling* 14, no. 1 (fall 1995).
Hermann, Richard. "Schizophrenia: Clinical Manifestations, Course, Assessment, and Diagnosis." UpToDate.Com, July 26, 2013. Accessed February 24, 2015 at http://www.uptodate.com/contents/schizophrenia-clinical-manifestations-course-assessment-and-diagnosis.
Tarrier, Nicolas. *Clinical Handbook of Psychotic Disorders*. New York City, NY: The Guilford Press, 2008.
Weisman de Mamani, Amy, et al. "A Randomized Clinical Trial to Test the Efficacy of a Family-Focused, Culturally Informed Therapy for Schizophrenia." *Journal of Family Psychology* 28, no. 6 (Dec. 2014) US: American Psychological Association: 801.

Chapter 6

Frances, Allen. *Saving Normal*. New York, NY: HarperCollins Publishers, 2013.

Chapter 7

Heartlight.Org. "Evening Devotion, Nov. 11th." Retrieved October 4, 2016 from www.heartlight.org/spurgeon/1111-pm.html.
Poetry Foundation. "If." Retrieved October 4 2016 from www.poetryfoundation.org/poems-and-poets/poems/detal/46473.
Wurmbrand, Richard. *Tortured for Christ*. Living Sacrifice Book Company, 1998.

About the Author

Adam Lambdin is recently married to Jenece, and they live in rural Missouri where Adam works retail at a local home improvement store as an assistant department manager in the plumbing department. Adam got his BA in Christian ministries from The Master's University in 2008. Adam was in the army reserve as a trainee very briefly, having graduated from boot camp at Fort Benning, Georgia. He was medically discharged for schizophrenia and moved on to other things. Several years later, he became a certified teacher in the state of Missouri. He quit teaching and started in retail where he now works, but he has an ambition to teach in some capacity after he gets his master's of arts in biblical studies from his alma mater and continues to grow in the retail industry as well. Adam has a passion for education and wouldn't mind it if he had the option of going to school his whole life, if such a thing were possible and he had his wife's permission. He still loves baseball, specifically the Los Angeles Dodgers, and enjoys watching UFC fights with his brother, Avery, who is a jiu-jitsu student. Adam dutifully takes his medicine prescribed by his VA doctor every night and knows that that is what makes him able to function. He hopes that this book might encourage other schizophrenics to follow their psychiatrist's advice and encourage pastors to work with psychiatrists, not against them.

Made in the USA
Middletown, DE
25 September 2018